Spiritual Applications of the Tabernacle

Witness Lee

Living Stream Ministry
Anaheim, CA • www.lsm.org

First Edition, December 1987.

ISBN 978-0-87083-376-2 (softcover)

Published by

Living Stream Ministry
2431 W. La Palma Ave., Anaheim, CA 92801 U.S.A.
P. O. Box 2121, Anaheim, CA 92814 U.S.A.

Printed in the United States of America

08 09 10 11 12 13 / 10 9 8 7 6 5 4

CONTENTS

PREFACE

This book is composed of messages given by Brother Witness Lee in the spring of 1963 in Los Angeles, California.

CHAPTER ONE

THE SABBATH AND
THE REVELATION OF THE TABERNACLE

Scripture Reading: Exo. 31:12-17

Exodus 25:1—31:11 contains the revelation of God to Moses concerning all the matters of the tabernacle and its service. Immediately following this is God's further word on the Sabbath. Since God's word on the Sabbath was written as the conclusion of all the revelations in the preceding chapters, it must surely be significant. In Genesis 1, after all things had been created in six days, there was the Sabbath on the seventh day. In the same way, after all things were revealed to Moses concerning the Lord's work and the services of the tabernacle, the Lord reminded the people of Israel to keep the Sabbath. After all the divine work there is the Sabbath.

THE PRINCIPLE OF THE SABBATH

We must consider the principle and the meaning of the Sabbath. For six days God worked in creation. After God had done everything and all things were completed, accomplished, and finished, He kept the Sabbath. Therefore, the Sabbath is the result of God's work. In this result, that is, on the Sabbath day, God rested. Exodus 31:17 says, "It is a sign between Me and the children of Israel forever; for in six days Jehovah made heaven and earth, and on the seventh day He rested and was refreshed." God not only needs to rest but also to be refreshed. The result of the divine work, which is the Sabbath, was that God could rest and refresh Himself. This result was an enjoyment for God, and God rejoiced in this result.

After we have finished a certain work, we then enjoy it. This is especially true with the sisters who cook. After they have done everything in their kitchen, they sit down at the table and enjoy what they have done. The table is the "Sabbath" to them. They sit there, enjoy it, and are refreshed. However, after a mother has finished her cooking, she does not go to the table by herself. She goes to the table with her children. The table is not an enjoyment to her alone; it is an enjoyment to her with her children. Without her children she could not rest. Even though the cooking is completed and the whole table is prepared, could a proper mother sit down, eat well, and enjoy rest and refreshment if her children were missing? The table is not for the mother alone but is for her and her children. On the first Sabbath day, after the conclusion of the creation, God did not rest alone. All creation rested with Him, and God especially rested with the man He created.

To God the Sabbath was the seventh day. To man, however, the Sabbath was the first day. Man was the final item of God's creation and was created on the sixth day, probably toward the end of the sixth day. Therefore, immediately after man had been created, he entered into the Sabbath. All the divine work was done by God. Nothing was done by man. Therefore, the Sabbath is the result of the divine work and is the rest to God with man. Man's obligation to God is not to work but to enjoy. The obligation of the work has been borne by God already. God's portion is to work and enjoy, but man's portion is simply to enjoy.

However, after the enjoyment there is a further work. After Adam had been created by God, he entered into the Sabbath, the first day to him, to rest and to enjoy. But after that day he began to work, to till the ground (Gen. 2:15). With God, work is first and enjoyment is second. With man, enjoyment is first and work is second. This is the vision of the principle of grace. God did the work and then enjoyed. We enjoy what God has done; then we work.

Not only with creation but also with redemption it is the same. The Lord has accomplished everything for redemption. After the completion of His redemption the Lord enjoyed the result. The Lord worked first and enjoyed later. We, however, enjoy first and work later. Concerning redemption and grace, we have nothing to do. Everything is finished. We simply enter into the Lord's accomplishment and have our rest. To receive the gospel is to enter into the work which the Lord has finished. Take it as the Sabbath, as your rest, and enjoy it with the Lord. But after you enjoy it, you have to bear some obligation to work. After our enjoyment we should offer ourselves to the Lord to do His work.

CHRIST AS THE SABBATH

The result of God's work, especially in redemption, is Christ Himself. Christ is the Sabbath, and the Sabbath day typifies Christ. Therefore, when the Lord came in the flesh, He abolished the old Sabbath day (Matt. 12:1-12). God can rest and be refreshed only in Christ, with Christ, and with the redeemed ones. Without us to enjoy His rest, to be refreshed together with God, God cannot rest and be refreshed. The parable in Luke 15:11-32 indicates that without the prodigal son returning home, the father could not rest at his table to enjoy the feast. The father's table in Luke 15 is the Sabbath to the father and to the son. But without the son, the father could not rest and enjoy the table. That table is Christ Himself, for upon that table was the slain, fattened calf (v. 23), signifying the rich Christ (Eph. 3:8) killed on the cross for the believers' enjoyment. The Sabbath is Christ as the result of the divine work, especially in redemption. God enjoys resting and being refreshed in Christ and with Christ with all the redeemed ones. We, as the redeemed ones, as the spiritual Israel (Gal. 6:16), have to realize that everything has been accomplished by God. Nothing was done by us. We must now enter into God's accomplishment and refresh ourselves with God.

If we attempt to do what God has accomplished, we will bring in death. Exodus 31:15 says, "Whoever does any work on the Sabbath day shall surely be put to death." The Sabbath is the result of God's work. You must keep your hand off of this work. Stop yourself. Do not do anything but simply appreciate, adore, praise, and receive Christ as your Sabbath.

Enjoy Christ and rest and refresh yourself with God, in Christ and with Christ, in His all-inclusive work. Then God will be pleased with you. Otherwise, you will bring in death.

Death means that you are cut off from God as your portion and from the enjoyment of what God has done.

THE LORD'S DAY

We have pointed out that the principle of the Sabbath is that God works first and then enjoys what He has done, but man first enjoys what God is and what God has accomplished, and then he is enabled to work. It is not that we work first and then have the enjoyment but that we enjoy first and then work. This is the principle of grace, to receive salvation first and then work with and by this salvation.

Certain Christians, according to their natural concept, insist on keeping the Old Testament Sabbath, the seventh day. Actually, to keep the Sabbath according to the Old Testament is to observe it from Friday evening to Saturday evening and to abstain even from cooking meals (35:2-3). To practice this in the New Testament times is foolish. The significance of keeping the seventh day is that one works first and then has the Sabbath. But we, as believers in the New Testament time, have the Lord's Day first, and then we go to work. From a child I understood the Sunday of Christianity to be the seventh day. We called Monday the first day of the week, and Sunday was the seventh day, the "Sabbath." Later, the Lord pointed out to me that Sunday is not the last day of the seven days. The Lord's Day is the first day of the seven days. The week in the New Testament begins with the Lord's Day. The Lord's Day to us is not a day of pleasure or recreation but a day of enjoying the Lord and serving Him. The term *Sunday* is a pagan name, a name related to idol worship. But to us the first day is the Lord's Day (Rev. 1:10) because the Lord resurrected on this day (Matt. 28:1-6). It is not only the first day, but it is also the eighth day. The Lord passed through "one week" to accomplish redemption, and we receive what the Lord has accomplished on the eighth day, the day of resurrection, which is the first day of the week. This means that we began as Christians in the principle of resurrection.

According to the principle of salvation, we first come to enjoy the Lord and what He has accomplished. This is our Sabbath, our rest. At the conclusion of all the revelations concerning the tabernacle and the service, the Sabbath is mentioned. This is a sign to signify that God has taken care of all the work. There is nothing left for man to do. What man is obligated to do is to rest with God and enjoy what God has accomplished. Then after we have enjoyed, we work for God with what we have enjoyed. The grace enables us to serve the Lord.

CHAPTER TWO

THE SEPARATION
OF THE TENT AND THE CAMP

Scripture Reading: Exo. 33:1-11; Heb. 13:13

THE TESTIMONY OF GOD

In Exodus the Ten Commandments are called the tablets of the Testimony (32:15). The Ten Commandments were not merely a law given by God to test the people of Israel but were the testimony of God Himself. The commandments testify of God in two ways. First, they testify that God is the unique God (20:2-3). Besides Him there is no God. Only He Himself is the God who created the heavens and the earth. Secondly, they testify of the nature of God. God is a God of holiness and a God of justice and righteousness. He is a holy God and a righteous God. Therefore, His people have to conduct themselves in a way which corresponds to the nature of God. These are the two primary matters which are testified by the Ten Commandments. Exodus 32 records that before the Ten Commandments had been brought down from Mount Sinai by Moses, the entire company of the children of Israel made a golden calf under the leadership of Aaron (vv. 1-6). They worshipped the golden calf, and in doing so they broke the first aspect of the testimony of the law, that is, that God is the unique God.

The children of Israel had been called out by God to bear His testimony to all creation, especially to the angels, to the rulers and authorities in the heavenlies, to testify that God is the very unique God and that God is a God of holiness and righteousness. However, these people broke God's testament and put it aside. Exodus 32:6 says, "The people sat down to eat and drink and rose up to play." They even danced before the calf (v. 19). In this way they also broke the second aspect of the law, that is, that God is a God of holiness and righteousness. What they did was contrary to and could never correspond with God's holiness and righteousness. On the one hand, they made the idol, and on the other hand, they defiled themselves. They sinned by making and worshipping a graven image (20:4) and by conducting themselves contrary to God's nature. Thus, in the eyes of the Lord and in the eyes of Moses as well, they broke the whole testimony. Moses considered that there was no need to keep the two tablets of the Testimony. It was not merely Moses who broke the tablets at the foot of the mountain (32:19); it was the people of Israel who had broken the testimony already. The Lord's testimony had been thrown away and broken. What Moses did was to let the people of Israel know that they had absolutely broken the Lord's testimony. They had broken the entire law.

All these things concerning the children of Israel were written as examples to us (1 Cor. 10:6) and are therefore types which we must apply. The Lord has called the believers out of the world to be a testimony to Him (1 Pet. 2:9). We are a testimony that the Lord has given us Christ as our good land to be everything to us (Col. 2:6-7). In the New Testament times the church must be the testimony of the Lord, bearing His testimony to the entire universe, especially to the principalities and powers in the heavens. On the one hand, we testify that the Lord is the unique God, and on the other hand, we testify of the nature of the Lord. Therefore, we must be heavenly, spiritual, holy, and righteous because the nature of the Lord is heavenly, spiritual, holy, and righteous. We must keep ourselves in a condition that corresponds with the Lord's nature.

However, not very long after the apostles' time, the church, like the children of Israel, broke the entire testimony of the Lord. The Christians erected a "golden calf" in bringing many idolatrous things into the church. They likewise became loose by doing things against the nature of the Lord. Today's celebration of Christmas is an example of the name of Christ being used for the purpose of idolatry and human pleasure. Taking the name of Christ, many people attend dancing parties on Christmas Eve. The entire testimony of the Lord has been broken today.

After the golden calf was destroyed, Moses called those who would be faithful to the Lord to stand with the Lord and take up the sword to slay those who worshipped the idols and became loose (Exo. 32:25-29). The Levites were the over- comers who stood with Moses for the Lord's testimony to express that they did not go along with the idol worshippers. They were separated from the people to testify that the Lord was the supreme One, the one God, and that He was holy and righteous. They could not tolerate the idol worship and the looseness, so they purified themselves, and by doing so they gained the priesthood. On the one hand, God was for Israel. He was faithful to them and would not altogether forsake them. On the other hand, He could not give up His testimony. God's intention was to have the whole nation of Israel as His priests (19:6), but by breaking God's testimony they lost the priesthood. The Levites, however, received the priesthood by being faithful to the Lord's testimony.

THE PRESENCE OF THE LORD
AND THE FELLOWSHIP WITH THE LORD

After this, in Exodus 33 the Lord indicated that His pres- ence would not go with the children of Israel. He told them to depart and go into the promised land, adding, "I will send an Angel before you...For I will not go up in your midst,...for you are a stiff-necked people" (vv. 2-3). On the one hand, the Lord forgave the people of Israel, but on the other hand, He kept His presence from them. All but two of those Israelites fell in the wilderness and never went into the promised land. This was the judgment of the Lord. God is a God of mercy and love, but He is also a God of government. This portion of the Word warns us that the presence of the Lord would not be with a people who do not keep His testimony.

Before they made and worshipped the golden calf, the people of Israel as a whole were the unique realm and circle related to the Lord's presence (19:5-6). But after they made and worshipped the golden calf, a separation came into being.

Exodus 33:7 says, "Now Moses would take the tent and pitch it outside the camp, some distance from the camp; and he called it the tent of meeting. And everyone who sought Jehovah went out to the tent of meeting, which was outside the camp." The tent in this verse refers to the tent of Moses. Before this time the tent of Moses was always within the camp because the presence of the Lord was in the midst of the people of Israel. But because Moses realized that the Lord's presence would no longer be in the midst of the people, he removed his tent, which then became the tent of God, and pitched it outside the camp. This means that there was a separation between the tent where God was and the camp.

After Moses took and pitched the tent outside the camp, the pillar of cloud descended upon it (v. 9); that is, the presence of the Lord was with Moses at the tent. Any of the people who were seeking the Lord had to go outside the camp to the tent where Moses was. If the people would not go outside the camp but would remain in it, they would not have the presence of the Lord. The presence of the Lord would no longer be in the camp but would be in the tent.

There was a separation and a distinction between the tent and the camp. At the tent there was not only the presence of the Lord but also the fellowship of the Lord. Exodus 33:11 is the first verse in the Scriptures which says that the Lord spoke to Moses face to face as a man speaks to a companion. In order to have the presence of the Lord and the fellowship with the Lord, one had to leave the camp and be in the tent. Only at the tent was there the presence of the Lord and the fellowship with the Lord.

THE RELIGIOUS CAMP

The camp signifies a group of people, in particular, a religious people, who are not faithful to the Lord. They name the name of the Lord (2 Tim. 2:19), but in fact they worship idols. This is the meaning of the camp. The presence of the Lord would not be with such ones, and they could not have fellowship with the Lord.

When the Lord Jesus was on the earth there was a separation between the Jewish people, the camp, and the Lord

Himself, the real tabernacle (John 1:14; 2:19, 21). The Lord fully forsook His relationship with the Jews in the flesh (Matt. 12:46-50 and footnote 48[1]; 13:1 and footnote 1[1]). From the time of Matthew 12 the Lord gave up the Jewish religious camp and pitched the tent outside the camp. There became a separation between the Jewish religion (the camp) and the Lord. From that day the presence of God was not again with the Jewish religion, and from that day all those who remained in it lost the fellowship with the Lord.

Any of the Jewish people who would have the presence of the Lord and who would have the fellowship with the Lord had to leave Judaism, that is, go outside the camp unto Jesus, who was the real tabernacle with the presence of God and the fellowship with God. By the time the Lord was on the earth, Judaism had become a camp. As a religious group, in name they were the people of God and with their mouth they honored the Lord, but in fact, they worshipped something other than God Himself. Their hearts were set on something other than the Lord. In Matthew 15:8 the Lord said regarding the Jewish religionists, "This people honors Me with their lips, but their heart stays far away from Me." The Lord called them a stiff-necked people (Exo. 33:3; Acts 7:51). Therefore, the Lord took the tent and pitched it outside of Judaism, and there became a separation between Him and those within Judaism.

From this separation the church came into being, for after His forsaking of the house of Israel, He turned to another people. The church is the tabernacle, or temple, of God (Eph. 2:21-22). However, after a certain period of time, the church changed in nature from being the tent to being a camp. This means that the church degraded to become Christianity. In principle, Christianity as a religious system comprises a group of religious people, belonging to the Lord in name and honoring the Lord with their mouth, but having their hearts set on something other than the Lord. At this present time, Christianity is not a tent but a camp. According to the history of the church, those who really sought the Lord had to leave organized Christianity, that is, leave the camp and go forth unto the Lord outside the camp.

GOING FORTH UNTO HIM OUTSIDE THE CAMP

Hebrews 13:13 says, "Let us therefore go forth unto Him outside the camp, bearing His reproach." We must go out of the camp unto Jesus because Jesus has left the camp. Jesus was driven out of the camp and was put to death outside the camp. The camp would not accept Jesus the Lord. There was a religious group who had the Lord in name but worshipped something other than the Lord. They did not accept the Lord, and they even gave up the Lord. Therefore, the Lord gave them up. If we are going to have the presence and the fellowship of the Lord, we have to go out of the camp.

In the history of God's people the camp may be seen in at least three periods. The camp was first the children of Israel after they worshipped the idol in Exodus 32. They had the name of belonging to the Lord but in reality they worshipped something else and hence became a religious camp among whom it was impossible to have the Lord's presence. Second, the Jews in Judaism, the Jewish religion, became the camp at the time of the Lord's living on the earth. They also were a religious group, claiming the name of the Lord but worshipping something other than the Lord. Later, Christianity also became the camp, taking the name of the Lord but not worshipping the Lord in spirit and reality (John 4:24). The Lord's presence would not be in the camp. The Lord's presence left all the camps, and all those who really seek the Lord have to leave the camp, go out of the camp unto the Lord. Those who do will have the presence and the fellowship of the Lord. This is a very solemn matter.

We have to ask ourselves whether we are in the camp or in the tent, even whether we are the camp or the tent. At the very beginning of our practice of the church we stressed this matter very much. We have to go out of the camp unto the Lord. We cannot and we should not remain in Christianity as a religious camp. We left the denominations because we realized that all the denominations are simply a religious camp. In the eyes of the Lord, Christianity is a camp. Outside of the camp there is the tent of the Lord. Now we are not in the camp, and we are not the camp people. We are in the tent, and we even are the tent. We are people who have followed the Lord out of Christianity, outside the camp. However, we have to be very careful. It may be that after a certain period of time we also will become the camp.

What is the camp, and what is the tent? The camp is a religious people who belong to the Lord in name but who in actuality worship something and seek something other than the Lord; the tent is a separation from that religious group.

SEPARATION BUT NOT DIVISION

There is always the separation of the tent and the camp. We have to realize, however, that separation and division are different. Division between the Lord's people is something evil. Moses and Joshua were not divided from the Lord's people, but they were separated from them (Exo. 33:7-11). Likewise, we would never say that we have made a division among the Lord's people, but we would say and even insist that we must make a separation from the camp of Christianity. We cannot give up the separation, but we have no intention to make a division. We must differentiate between separation and division. If we are going to set up another sect, we will make a division, but we have no intention to do that. We would not be divided from the Lord's children, but Christianity has become a camp. Because the Lord has come out of it, we must also separate ourselves from the camp and set up the tent.

The tent and the camp are a clear picture of our real situation. Originally the camp was the place where the Lord's presence and fellowship were, but at a certain point it lost its nature and became idolatrous. Therefore, the people who know the Lord's heart must leave it and set up a tent. Immediately after Moses pitched the tent, the pillar of cloud descended to the entrance of the tent, and Jehovah spoke to Moses as a companion, face to face (33:9-11). All those who are seeking the Lord have to go outside the camp and go forth unto Him at the tent.

CHAPTER THREE

THE TENT OF MEETING, THE SERVICE, AND THE PRIESTLY GARMENTS

Scripture Reading: Exo. 35:20—36:1

Exodus 35 through 39 is a record of the building of the tabernacle, its furniture, and the priestly garments. Chapter 35, as the first chapter in this section, is full of spiritual meaning. If we enter into it in a full way, we will realize that it is very rich. This portion of the Word shows us how the building of the Lord, the service to the Lord, and the fellowship between the Lord and His people can be built up.

Exodus 35:21 says, "They...brought the heave offering of Jehovah for the work of the Tent of Meeting and for all its service and for the holy garments." Three items are mentioned here—the Tent of Meeting, the service, and the holy garments. The Tent of Meeting differs slightly in meaning from the tabernacle. The tabernacle refers to the dwelling place of God, whereas the Tent of Meeting refers not only to the dwelling place of God but also to the place where the people of God meet together with God. The place where God dwells is the place where the people of God meet together. What the people of Israel were to build up was a tent, which was, on the one hand, the dwelling place of God, and on the other hand, a place, a center, where they could meet together before God and with God. This is a picture of the church life. The church, which is the house of God (1 Tim. 3:15), is the dwelling place of God and the place where all the children of God meet together before God and with God. The tent was the first item that they were to build up.

The second item in Exodus 35:21 is the service of the Tent of Meeting. With the dwelling place of God where the people of God meet together there is always the service of God. Whenever we come together with God and before God, there is always the service. The service at that time among the people of Israel mostly depended on the oil and the incense (v. 28). The oil refers to the Holy Spirit, and the incense signifies the resurrection of Christ. This means that all the service must be something of the Holy Spirit and of the resurrection of Christ. The service to God and of God, the genuine service, the real service to the Lord, must be something built up by the people of God. Not only the building, the house of God, has to be built by the people of God, but even the service to God has to be built up by us.

The third item in verse 21 is the holy garments. The holy garments represent the priestly ministry, or the priesthood, and the priestly ministry was the fellowship between the people of God and the Lord Himself. Between God Himself and the people of Israel there was a priesthood, a priestly ministry. Everything in this ministry was contained in the garments with which the priest was clothed. The relationship between God and His people absolutely depended on the priesthood, and the garments of the priest represented that priestly ministry. Therefore, the garments here represent the fellowship between the Lord's people and the Lord Himself. Without the priestly garments there could be no priesthood, and without the priesthood there could be no relationship between God and His people. The holy garments as the fellowship between God and His people also have to be built up.

What we are building up today is of three items. We must build up the dwelling place of God where we can meet with each other before God and with God. We must also build up the service to God. Something in the Holy Spirit and in the resurrected life of Christ must be built up by us in coordination. The service to God is not natural but is something in the Holy Spirit and in the resurrection of Christ to be built up by the experiences of God's children, God's people. We must also build up a fellowship between God's people and God Himself. These three items have to be built up by the experiences of the Lord's children. If we have no experience of the spiritual life, we will have nothing with which to build, and we will not know how to build. We must have the material and the gifts (vv. 21-29) with which to build, and we must have the wisdom, the way, to know how to build (vv. 25-26, 31, 35). The dwelling place of God, the service of God, and the fellowship with God have to be built up by the experiences of the Lord's children.

THE MATERIALS FOR THE BUILDING

Exodus 35 speaks of the different materials offered by the people of God for the building of the tabernacle. All these materials offered by the people of Israel represent the things of Christ which were experienced by the people of God. They experienced these items, so they possessed them. What they offered were the things which they possessed, earned, and had in their hands. The things experienced and possessed by them they now brought to offer to God to be the material for the building.

Articles of Gold

The items offered by the people are listed in six categories. The first category is the articles of gold (vv. 5, 22). Gold in type represents the divine nature, that is, God Himself. Each child of God has something of gold, something of God's nature. There is not one exception. With the other categories of materials, some shared in them, and others did not. But with this first category of the offerings, everyone had a share. Exodus 35:22 says, "They came, men together with women, as many as were of a willing heart, and brought nose rings and earrings and signet rings and pendants, all kinds of articles of gold; even every man who waved a wave offering of gold to Jehovah." This means that every saved one, every one of God's children, has something of God's divine nature. The nose rings, earrings, signet rings, and pendants represent the ornaments of the Lord's children, consisting of the divine nature which we have experienced.

Because we have the experiences of the divine nature, we can have something to offer to God for His building. Without the experiences of God's divine life and nature, we would have nothing to offer to God for His building. With what shall we build the church? We are building the church with God's divine nature. First Corinthians 3:12 says that we build the church with gold, silver, and precious stones. When the divine life and nature become our experience, we have something to offer to the Lord as material for His building. The more we experience God's nature, the more we will have to offer to the Lord as material for His building. We are building the church, not with mere humanity or human things but with gold, with the divine nature, which we have experienced, which we possess, and which we have in our hands as our wealth.

Weaving Materials

The second category of materials are the weaving materials, such as the blue, purple, and scarlet strands, fine linen, and the other materials for the coverings, the goats' hair, rams' skins dyed red, and porpoise skins (Exo. 35:6, 7a, 23). These represent the things which the Holy Spirit has "woven," or wrought, into us. Blue represents heavenliness, purple represents authority and kingship, and scarlet represents redemption, the redeeming power. Furthermore, fine linen represents the righteousness of God which is Christ Himself, the goats' hair represents Christ enduring the judgment of God, and the porpoise skins represent Christ as the power to endure the sufferings of human life. The porpoise skins were the outermost covering of the tabernacle (36:19) and protected the tabernacle from the sunshine, wind, rain, and all manner of attacks. They represent the enduring power, strength, and energy of Christ to suffer all kinds of attacks during His human life on earth. All these things—the heavenliness, the kingship and authority, the redeeming power, the strength to endure the divine government and judgment, and the strength, the power, to suffer all manner of attacks—the Holy Spirit will work into us. These items will gradually be wrought into us by the Holy Spirit and woven into our life so that we may offer them to God as materials to build up the fellowship between God and His people for the Lord's service. The weaving materials are mainly for the fellowship because these materials pertain mostly to the priestly garments. Even the coverings of the tabernacle are actually related to the garments. The items of the weaving materials are also things which we experience. The more we experience the work of the Holy Spirit to weave something into us, the more we will have to offer to the Lord as the materials for the Lord's fellowship.

Silver and Bronze

The third category of the offerings is the silver and bronze (35:5, 24a). Silver represents the redemption of the cross, and bronze represents the judgment and the testing of God and even the trials from the enemy. We have to experience the redemption, the cross of Christ, and we have to experience the judgment and testing that Christ endured and suffered. Then the silver and bronze will become our possession, and we can offer them to the Lord for His building.

Acacia Wood

The fourth category of materials is the acacia wood (vv. 7b, 24b). Acacia wood represents renewed humanity. The tabernacle was made mainly with acacia wood overlaid with gold. This points to the human nature of the Lord Jesus, not the fallen human nature. This is human nature which is good for God's building. With us, this must be the human nature renewed, the human nature transformed. We are fallen people with the fallen nature. This fallen nature, our humanity or human nature, has to be renewed. If we are going to have God's building built among us, each one of us must have the proper human nature, or character. The renewed humanity, signified by the strong and durable acacia wood, is the material for the building of God.

One may be loose and lazy in his fallen nature and character. However, after he has been saved, this one will gradually be renewed by the resurrection life in the Holy Spirit. Through the resurrection life his character changes, and his human nature is transformed into something new. He becomes so strong and strict in his character. Such a humanity can be used as material for the building of God's dwelling place. The building of the church needs the renewed and transformed humanity as the basic material. If our nature, our character, still remains in the fallen condition and the old state, we can never be used as material for the building of the church. Thus, we have to be transformed and renewed in our humanity, our character, and human nature. Then we will become acacia wood for the building of the Lord's church.

Precious Stones

The fifth category is the onyx stones and the other precious stones (vv. 9, 27). The precious stones represent the work of the Holy Spirit through our circumstances. Precious stones are not in the original creation of God but are created things that have been burned and pressed to be changed into precious stones. This indicates that the Holy Spirit will work on us through the arrangement of certain circumstances and environments to "burn" us and to "press" us so that we may be transformed into precious stones.

Spices and Oil

The sixth category is the spices and oil (vv. 8, 28). Oil, representing the Holy Spirit, is for anointing, and spices, representing the resurrection of Christ, are for the incense. The resurrection of Christ always goes with the Holy Spirit. Without the Holy Spirit the resurrection of Christ could never be realized. The oil and the spices, the anointing and the incense, always go together. These things need to be experienced by the people of God so that they may possess all these things as their wealth. When the Lord had need of these items in Exodus, the people had them to offer to Him as the material for His building.

We must experience the Lord in many items. Then we also will be rich in what we possess, and we will be able to offer them to the Lord for His building. All the materials for the building of God were experienced and possessed by God's people. They had all these things in their hands, and these became their possession, their wealth, for them to offer to the Lord as material for His building.

The building of the church, the building up of the service of God, and the building up of the fellowship between the Lord's children and the Lord Himself must be with the Christ experienced and possessed by us to be our wealth. Then we bring all that we have experienced and possessed to offer to the Lord as the material for the building up of the dwelling place of God where we could meet together, for the building up of the service to the Lord, and for the building up of the fellowship between the Lord and His children.

CHAPTER FOUR

THE MATERIALS AND WORKMANSHIP IN GOD'S BUILDING

(1)

Scripture Reading: Exo. 35:22-35; 36:1-7

Exodus 35 and 36 reveal to us the materials and the workmanship of the building of God. All these materials, as well as the service of the tabernacle, typify the things of Christ. By this we know that for the building of the Lord both the material and the workmanship must be something of Christ which we experience.

THE ASCENDED CHRIST AS THE HEAVE OFFERING

Verses 21 and 24 of Exodus 35 and verses 3 and 6 of chapter 36 refer to the heave offering. Exodus 35:21 reads, "They came, everyone whose heart lifted him up and everyone whose spirit made him willing, and brought the heave offering of Jehovah for the work of the Tent of Meeting and for all its service and for the holy garments." According to the original Hebrew language, the offering here is the heave offering. Verse 24a continues, "Everyone who offered a heave offering of silver and bronze brought the heave offering of Jehovah." *Offered,* here, should be translated as "heaved." Verse 3a in chapter 36 says, "They received from Moses every heave offering which the children of Israel had brought for the work of the service of the sanctuary, to make it." Verse 6b reads, "Let neither man nor woman produce any more material for the heave offering of the sanctuary."

These verses tell us that all the materials used for the building of the Tent of Meeting, its service, and the holy garments of the priests were heave offerings, offered or heaved, by the people of Israel. The word *heave* means "to lift up," indicating that Christ has been lifted up into the heavens. The heave offering typifies the ascended Christ, the Christ ascended to the heavens.

The ascension of Christ into the heavens is the climax, the highest peak, of Christ's experience. Before the ascension there were many things related to Christ, and after the ascension there are more matters related to Christ, but all these, whether before the ascension or after the ascension, are included in the Christ typified by the heave offering. The things of Christ before the ascension began from eternity past. Christ was the very God in eternity past. He was the Word of God (John 1:1), the explanation of God. He accomplished the creation of the heavens and of the earth and of all things within the universe (v. 3; Col. 1:16). Then He was incarnated to be a man (John 1:14) and lived on this earth for thirty-three and a half years. When He was on this earth, He experienced human living and all the sufferings and hardships of human life. He went to the cross to be crucified, to enter into death, and He was buried and went into Hades (Phil. 2:8; Acts 2:23, 27). He was raised up from Hades and the grave, and He was lifted up to the third heavens (vv. 24, 31-35). By this, He reached the highest point of the universe; that is, He ascended to the heaven of heavens.

Then, after the ascension, He sent down the Holy Spirit; that is, He came down from the heavens as the Holy Spirit (John 14:16, 18) to visit His redeemed ones and enter into them to be their resurrection life and their all. He Himself came as the Spirit and entered into us to transform us into a fully renewed new man (Eph. 4:23-24), the fullness of Himself, which is His Body, the church (1:22-23).

The church came into being due to His descension as the Holy Spirit after His ascension. In the period between His ascension and eternity future He accomplishes many spiritual things, including the regeneration, transformation, and renewing of the church as His full expression.

After the completion of the renewing of the new man and the building up of His Body, eternity future will begin. He will be the center of that eternal age. All these matters are included in the ascended Christ. This ascended Christ is the heave offering, and all the people of God offered something of this ascended Christ for the building of God. Whatever they offered is referred to as the heave offering.

The Christ in whom we believe is not only the Christ who was born of a virgin and who died for us. The Christ in whom we believe, whom we receive as our life and we enjoy as our all, is the Christ who has ascended to the heavens. All the things offered by the people of God for God's building were something of the ascended Christ. Therefore, they are called the heave offering. We also need to experience and enjoy Him as the ascended Christ for the building of God.

THE ITEMS OF THE HEAVE OFFERING
AND THE WAVE OFFERING

The Wave Offering of Gold

We have seen that the things offered by the people are of six categories. The first category is the articles of gold. Exodus 35:22 says, "They came, men together with women, as many as were of a willing heart, and brought nose rings and earrings and signet rings and pendants, all kinds of articles of gold; even every man who waved a wave offering of gold to Jehovah." Gold signifies the divine nature of Christ. The divine life and nature are the first item we experience of Christ. As long as we are regenerated by Christ, we have the divine nature and the divine life of God (2 Pet. 1:4; John 3:15-16). This is the first item of the riches of Christ that we possess by experiencing Him. If you do not have this, you have not yet been saved. If you have been saved, you at least have this item of spiritual wealth.

The gold here is not something hidden or covered. It is something manifested as your beauty. The articles of gold in Exodus 35:22 are the ornaments worn on the exposed parts of the body, such as the face, neck, and arms. This signifies that the divine nature and the divine life of God in Christ are now manifested upon you as your beauty. People could see and realize that in you there is the divine beauty of the divine life and nature.

Our experience of the divine life and nature are in resurrection. Therefore, the offerings of gold are the wave offerings (v. 22). The meaning of the wave offering is different from that of the heave offering. To wave implies movement and means that you are living, you are alive. When you come to the meeting, you must "wave." You should not sit or stand still; you must have some "motion." Whenever we come together and a brother or a sister offers a prayer or gives a testimony, we may say that they are waving a wave offering. All the beauties of God's divine nature which are manifested upon us must be something alive, something living and full of life. They are not dead or motionless but full of life, full of motion and action. When we love a brother or do something in the resurrection life of the Lord Jesus, there is the beauty of life full of "motion." This is something done in the resurrection power of the life of God. This is the manifestation of the divine life and nature.

Because we experience the divine life and nature, we have the surplus of the divine life and nature as the wealth in our hands. Then we can bring this to wave to the Lord as the wave offering for the building of the Lord.

The Coverings

The second item of the offerings is the coverings, whether for the covering of the tent or for the clothing for the priests. Exodus 35:23 says, "Every man with whom was found blue and purple and scarlet strands and fine linen and goats' hair and rams' skins dyed red and porpoise skins brought them." The coverings were mostly of the woven materials. Although it does not clearly mention whether these are called the heave offering or the wave offering, we must realize that these are surely something of the heave offering. All these materials are something of the ascended Christ.

Verse 23 mentions the heavenly color, blue; the color of kingship, purple; the color of redemption, scarlet; and the color of Christ as righteousness, white, as implied by fine linen. All these characteristics of the ascended Christ, the heavenly Christ, have to be woven into our life. In this way all these characteristics will be a covering to the Lord's people, who should be the priests serving God. The entire tent as well as the priesthood is covered with these characteristics. The fellowship between God and His people as signified by the priestly garments with the breastplate and shoulder plates also depends on these coverings. The coverings were woven of these materials, which are the various heavenly aspects and characteristics of Christ.

The blue, purple, scarlet, and white threads were of linen, something of the vegetable life, and the goats' hair, the rams' skins dyed red, and the porpoise skins were of the animal life. The animal life signifies the redeeming aspect of Christ as our life. Christ gave up His life to suffer judgment, punishment, and death. He also suffered the attacks and trials from man and Satan, and the tests from God. All these sufferings of Christ for redemption are typified by the animal life. The porpoise skins are for protection and typify Christ as the One who has the strength and the energy to suffer and endure all kinds of attacks. Christ as the porpoise skins can withstand every attack, whether from people or from the evil spirits. Christ can endure any kind of circumstance. We must experience the ascended Christ in this aspect.

Silver and Bronze as the Heavenly Foundation and Protection

The third item of offerings is the silver and bronze, or copper (v. 24a). This item in verse 24 is called the heave offering. Although the offerings of gold are called the wave offering, the things of silver and bronze are referred to as the heave offering because they represent something of the heavenly authority. Silver is for the base, the support, and the foundation of the Tent of Meeting. The sockets as the foundation of the tent were made of silver (36:24, 26, 30).

The bronze is in the same principle. The hangings for the outer court were placed upon the base of bronze (38:11, 17). The bronze was for the foundation as a protection for the tent. For God's building to have a proper foundation, there must be the heavenly authority. If there is no authority, there is no foundation or protection. All the silver and the bronze are for the foundation as the protection to the tent, and this foundation and protection must be something heavenly. It is a foundation on the earth, but it is a heavenly foundation, representing the heavenly foundation and protection to the church on this earth. The heavenly characteristics of Christ become the foundation as a protection to the church.

Acacia Wood as the Human Character of the Ascended Christ

The fourth item of the offerings is acacia wood (35:24b), typifying the human character of the ascended Christ. We have to experience the character of the ascended Christ, which on the one hand is a human character and on the other hand is a resurrected, ascended, and heavenly character. Our character today has to be transformed and renewed into the likeness of the ascended Christ.

Precious Stones as the Solid and Deeper Experiences of Christ

The fifth item is the precious stones (v. 27). These are offered by the leaders, the principal ones among the Lord's children, who have the authority. These precious stones are something related to those who have authority. This means that if you are going to be one with authority among the Lord's children, you have to have something to offer to the Lord as precious stones. If you do not have this kind of wealth, you cannot take the lead among the Lord's children. To have something of the precious stones means that in your life, in your spiritual experience, you have suffered the burning and the pressure. Thus, with you there is something very solid, very strong, and very precious, like precious stones. These experiences are much deeper than the experiences of the articles of gold. The precious stones typify the deeper and further experiences of Christ. If we have something precious of Christ as the precious stones, we have the authority. Then we will be ones who can take the lead among the Lord's children.

Spices and Oil as the Resurrected and Ascended Christ

The sixth item is the spices and oil (v. 28). As we have seen, the spices represent the sweet odor of the resurrection life of Christ. The resurrection life of Christ is so sweet to God. The oil represents the Holy Spirit, and this Holy Spirit is related to the resurrection of Christ. The resurrected Christ is the Christ who became the Spirit (1 Cor. 15:45b). The spices and the oil represent Christ resurrected and ascended to God and coming down to visit people to enable people to serve God. All the services offered by men to God are included in the spices and the oil. The spices are for the slain and resurrected Savior, the sweet odor offered to God, and the oil represents the Holy Spirit in whom we can render the service to God. The spices and oil are offered not by the people but by the leaders of the people. Only those who could offer the precious stones could offer spices and oil. This is quite meaningful. Only when one has the deeper and further experiences of Christ as the precious stones could he offer the spices and the oil. Because he is so matured, so full of the Holy Spirit, he can offer the spices and the oil. All these are the items of the offerings and are called the heave offering, something of the ascended and heavenly Christ.

CHAPTER FIVE

THE MATERIALS AND WORKMANSHIP IN GOD'S BUILDING

(2)

Scripture Reading: Exo. 35:25—36:7

THE ORDER OF THE OFFERED MATERIALS

The order in which the materials for the building are mentioned in Exodus 35:22-29 is very significant. The first category of materials is the ornaments made of gold (v. 22). As we have seen, this category represents the experiences of the divine nature of Christ. This is the beginning of all our spiritual experiences.

The Detailed Experiences

The second category is the weaving materials and the coverings for the tabernacle. Exodus 35:23 says, "Every man with whom was found blue and purple and scarlet strands and fine linen and goats' hair and rams' skins dyed red and porpoise skins brought them." Silver and bronze, the third category, and acacia wood, the fourth category, are mentioned in verse 24. However, following this, verses 25 and 26 again speak of the woven materials. We must have the experiences of the weaving materials in a more detailed way. Verses 25 and 26 say that the weaving materials—the blue, the purple, and the scarlet strands, the fine linen, and the goats' hair—had to be spun by the women. The aspects and characteristics of Christ typified by the weaving materials have to be experienced by us in a very detailed way. We must labor by the Holy Spirit to experience Christ as our righteousness, the heavenliness of

Christ, the kingship of Christ, and the redemption of Christ. Then these characteristics of Christ will be subjectively "spun" into us, and Christ will be wrought into our being in our experience. We should not view the heavenliness of Christ, the kingship of Christ, the authority of Christ, the redemption of Christ, or Christ as our righteousness in an objective way. All these are very subjective and must be experienced by us. We must labor to "spin" all these characteristics of Christ so that they may be subjectively ours as the material which we could offer to the Lord for His building.

We may know what the heavenliness, the kingship, the authority, and the redemption of Christ are. We may also know what it means for Christ to be righteousness to us. However, we need to experience all these matters. We need to spend our energy to labor on these things so that they will all become something belonging to us as our wealth. Even though the weaving materials in verse 23 are listed as the second category of materials, they are repeated in verses 25 and 26 after the silver, the bronze, and the acacia wood. The experience of the weaving materials is more subjective than the experiences of the silver, the bronze, and even the acacia wood.

The acacia wood is listed as the fourth category of materials in verse 24b. We have pointed out that acacia wood refers to our transformed character. The experience of the transformed character is more subjective than the experience of the silver, Christ's redemption, and the bronze, the judgment and test which Christ suffered. To experience Christ as our transformed character for the renewing and transformation of our human nature, our human character, is more subjective than the experiences of the silver and the bronze, which represent the foundation and the safeguard of the building.

The Most Subjective Experiences

The order of the offered materials is arranged in such a way as to list the most subjective things at the end. According to spiritual experience, the experience of the last two categories, the precious stones (v. 27) and the spices and oil (v. 28), are the most subjective. Verse 27 says that these last two categories of materials were offered by the leaders. The leaders signify the mature ones who have a certain degree of authority among the Lord's children. The "leaders" are more mature and have the most subjective experiences of the spiritual life.

The precious stones were offered for the fellowship of God with His people, but the oil and spices were offered for the service to God. The precious stones were materials for the breastplate and the ephod (v. 27), which were part of the priests' garments. The breastplate was the instrument by which the priests could contact God and have fellowship with God and could know the mind, the thought, and the will of God. Thus, it represents the fellowship between the people of God and God Himself. This fellowship is based upon the precious experiences of the matured persons. If among us there were not a group of matured ones with such subjective experiences, we could not have much real fellowship with God. In order to have a real fellowship with God among us, we need certain ones who are very mature and have the subjective experiences as the precious stones. We need the subjective and precious experiences as the precious stones to offer to the Lord as materials to build an instrument for the fellowship with the Lord. The fellowship with the Lord among His children is based upon the experiences of the mature ones.

The leaders also offered the spices and oil for the service to the Lord (v. 28). The spices are for incense, whereas the oil is for the light of the lamp and the holy anointing oil. To light the lamp, to anoint the persons and items related to the tabernacle, and to burn the incense are the main items of the service to the Lord. In order to have the service of the Lord, we must have the oil for the lighting and for the anointing, and we must have the spices for the incense to be burned before the Lord. We have seen that incense signifies the resurrection of Christ, and the oil represents the Holy Spirit. We must experience the resurrection of Christ and the Spirit of Christ to such an extent that we could have something to offer to the Lord for His service.

The tent, the fellowship, and the service are all constituted of the experiences of Christ by the Lord's children. Whether we shall have the real Tent of Meeting, the real fellowship with the Lord among us, and the real service to the Lord depends on our experiences of Christ. Without the experiences of Christ, we will be poor and will have nothing to offer to the Lord as the materials to build up these basic matters. The more we experience Christ, the more materials we will have, and the more the Tent of Meeting, the dwelling place of God, the fellowship, and the service will be built up among us.

THE WORKMANSHIP FOR GOD'S BUILDING

All the materials offered by the people for the building of the tabernacle typify something of Christ experienced by us. However, in order to have the building, the skillful workers and the workmanship are also needed (vv. 10, 30-35; 36:1-2). As we shall see, the workmanship for God's building is also Christ Himself experienced by us.

Being Filled with Christ as Our Wisdom

In Exodus 35 and 36 the workmanship is related to wisdom (35:31, 35; 36:1-2). Exodus 36:1-2 speaks of "every man who is wise in heart, in whom Jehovah has put wisdom." The heart of these workers was full of wisdom. Wisdom is simply Christ (1 Cor. 1:30). To have wisdom is to have the ability to know and understand spiritual matters and to know how to carry out matters. Therefore, wisdom, strictly speaking, is Christ as the way. If you have Christ, you have the way to know matters, understand matters, and know how to do things. Christ is our way. We must have Christ a
nd be filled with Christ.

With the building of the church and with the service of the Lord, there is the need of the experience of Christ, and there is the need of being filled with Christ. Our heart has to be filled with Christ. Then we will have the wisdom to know how to serve the Lord and how to build the church. The wisdom, the way for us to serve the Lord and to build the church, is Christ Himself. The spinning women in Exodus 35:25-26 and the skillful men in 36:1-2 were all filled in their hearts with wisdom; that is, their hearts were filled with Christ.

Four Steps in the Workmanship

Exodus 35:31 says of Bezalel, a principal worker for the

tabernacle, "He has filled him with the Spirit of God, with wisdom, with understanding, and with knowledge, and with all kinds of workmanship." This verse implies four steps. The first step, being filled with the Spirit of God, with wisdom, is in our spirit and our heart. When our spirit and our heart are filled with Christ, Christ becomes the wisdom in our spirit and heart. If we are going to serve the Lord in the church, that is, if we are going to have a share in the building of the church, our spirit and heart must firstly be filled with Christ.

From our spirit Christ will expand to our mind, our mentality. Christ will become our understanding in the second step. Wisdom is mainly in our spirit, but understanding is something in our mind. In our mentality we will understand the things concerning the service and the building. After we have understanding, we will have general knowledge, the third step. Spontaneously, we will have the knowledge and will know how to serve and how to build up the church.

Finally, after we have general knowledge, we will have the workmanship. We will have the divine idea of what to do and what to make. We will know what the shape, form, and style of our work should be. We may feel to visit the brothers and sisters. If we have the manner of workmanship, we will have a proper idea of how to visit them and a proper idea of what we are going to build by visiting them. We will have the proper form, style, and expression.

The order in verse 31 is significant. First, Christ fills our spirit and heart, and we have Him as our wisdom. Then He expands into our mentality, and we have the understanding in our mind. After we have the understanding in our mind, we have a general knowledge. Then we know how to function, how to fellowship with others, and how to visit the brothers and sisters. We know how to help the saints to make a clearance of their past, offer themselves to the Lord, and follow the consciousness of the inner life. We know as well how to help the saints to have a prayer life and study the Scriptures. We do not work blindly, not knowing what we are going to build. We know the style, the expression, and the shape of what we are building because we have the manner of workmanship.

We know what the need of the brothers and sisters is at the present time, we know how to help them, and we know by helping them what we shall be building.

Able to Teach Others

A person with all kinds of workmanship will also be able to teach others. Exodus 35:34 says, "He has put in his heart to teach." We must experience Christ beyond what is needed for us to conduct the spiritual work ourselves, to the extent that we can share with others and teach others. In the building of the church there is the need for us to teach others to do the same thing as we are able to do. The apostle Paul told Timothy to teach those who will be competent to teach others also (2 Tim. 2:2). We ourselves have to serve and build, but at the same time we must have wisdom, understanding, knowledge, and all kinds of workmanship to be competent to teach others, to help others to be able to serve as we serve and to build as we build.

Fashioning Skillful Designs

Exodus 35:32 says that the workers could fashion skillful designs. This is not the general kind of workmanship but rather something special. To fashion skillful, artistic designs requires additional wisdom. In the service and in the building of the church there is sometimes the need to fashion something artistic and skillful.

Verses 32 and 33 say, "To fashion skillful designs, to work in gold, and in silver and in bronze, and in the cutting of stones for setting and in the carving of wood, to work in all kinds of skillful workmanship." To work in gold we must know how to work with the divine nature of Christ. To work in silver we must know how to work with the redemption of Christ, with the cross, with the death of Christ. And to work in bronze, we must know how to work with the judgment, the tests, and the sufferings that the Lord endured. We must also know how to work in the cutting of stones for setting, that is, with the precious, deep, and most subjective experiences of Christ as the precious stones. We must also know how to work in the carving of wood. This means we must know how to work with the human character to make something out of it for the Lord's building.

Verse 35 goes on to say, "He has filled them with wisdom of heart, to work all kinds of workmanship, of an engraver and of a skillful workman and of an embroiderer in blue and in purple and in scarlet strands and in fine linen, and of the weaver, even of those who do all kinds of workmanship and of those who fashion skillful designs." We need to know how to embroider with the heavenliness of Christ, with the kingship, the authority, of Christ, with the redemption of Christ, and with Christ as our righteousness. We should know not only how to "spin," but also how to "weave." To spin is to make the thread from fiber, but to weave is to use the thread to make cloth.

If we spend some time to consider these matters, I believe that the Holy Spirit will speak more to us. What is presented in these verses is a full picture of the work of the building of the church. The way to build the church and to serve the church in the Lord is exactly as depicted by this picture. Sometimes we have to know how to work in gold, that is, with the divine nature of Christ. Sometimes we need to know how to work with silver and with bronze, and sometimes we need to know how to engrave, how to cut, or how to carve. Sometimes we need to know how to spin with the heavenliness of Christ, the authority of Christ, or with the redemption of Christ, and sometimes we need to know how to weave with Christ as our righteousness.

I believe that in these last days these experiences of Christ will be recovered among us. Many skillful men and women will be produced among us. Many will be spiritually skillful to work for the building of the Lord's dwelling place.

CHAPTER SIX

THE COVERING OF THE TABERNACLE

Scripture Reading: Exo. 36:8-19

Exodus 36:8-19 describes the coverings of the tabernacle. The coverings are the safeguard, the protection, of the tabernacle. Without the coverings, the tabernacle would have had no protection. It would have been exposed to the sunshine, to the wind, to the rain, and to all kinds of attacks. However, under the covering the tabernacle and all the things within the tabernacle were protected.

All the coverings are types of Christ. The tabernacle represents the dwelling place of God, which is the church. Christ is the covering, the safeguard, the protection, of the church. Furthermore, this Christ is not objective but is very subjective. The Christ whom we experience in different ways becomes the protection of the church.

The materials which compose the four layers of the coverings are the protection, the safeguard, of the church, but they all have to be experienced by us. If we experience the endurance and suffering strength of Christ typified by the porpoise skins, then we will have something to offer to the Lord as the material to compose such a covering to protect the church. If we do not experience Christ in such a way, there will be no protection or safeguard for the church. Even though Christ in Himself is able to protect the church, we have to experience Him. If we experience Christ, then He will be the protection of the church. The more we experience the endurance and the suffering strength and energy of Christ, the more the church will be protected and safeguarded by Christ.

FINE TWINED LINEN

According to Exodus 36 there were four layers of coverings.

The first layer was a covering made of fine twined linen (v. 8). Being twined indicates that the linen was doubled in strength. Linen in type represents the righteousness which is Christ Himself (1 Cor. 1:30; Rev. 19:8). Christ Himself is our righteousness before God. He is the sinless One, the One who has no sin and who knows no sin (2 Cor. 5:21). As the righteous One, He Himself is our righteousness in the sight of God. Furthermore, this righteousness is double in strength, as indicated by the word *twined*.

The curtains were linen and of blue, purple, and scarlet strands. Blue represents heavenliness, purple represents the kingship, the authority, and scarlet represents redemption. In addition, according to Exodus 36:8, the curtains were embroidered with cherubim. Cherubim, in the Scriptures, are related to God's glory, God's building, and God's creation (25:20; Heb. 9:5; Ezek. 10:3-5, 18-19; Rev. 4:6-7; 5:8, 13; cf. Ezek. 1:5-10). Thus, they represent the glory of God manifested in the human nature of Christ.

The first layer of the coverings was ten curtains of fine twined linen in two sections of five curtains each, joined to one another (Exo. 36:8, 10). This corresponds to the Ten Commandments of the law. In the Ark of the Testimony, which was under the coverings, there were two tablets, and five commandments were written on each of them. This shows us that the righteous One, who is Christ Himself, corresponds absolutely with the law of God. What the law of God requires, Christ meets to the full extent. Christ, the righteous One, meets all the requirements of the law.

The number ten, divided into two groups of five, signifies responsibility in fullness. The ten virgins in Matthew 25 are divided into two groups of five. Five is composed of four, representing man as the leading one of the creation, and one, representing God the Creator. Man plus God the Creator becomes five, indicating that man added with God bears responsibility. Christ, the righteous One, bore the full responsibility to fulfill the requirement of the law of God.

Exodus 36:9 says, "The length of each curtain was twenty-eight cubits, and the width of each curtain, four cubits; all the curtains had the same measurement." Twenty-eight is composed of eight plus twenty. This is very meaningful. The number eight represents resurrection (Matt. 28:1; John 20:1—"the first day of the week" is the eighth day). Twenty is composed of two times ten. Two represents a testimony, and ten, as we have pointed out, indicates full responsibility. Here is the testimony of the full responsibility which Christ has borne. Twenty is also composed of four times five, showing that Christ is the One in creation (Col. 1:15) who bears all the responsibility to fulfill the requirement of God's righteousness. Twenty-eight may also be composed of four, representing the creature, times seven, representing perfection and completion. Christ, who is the righteous One and who is our righteousness before God, took the full responsibility as the One in creation to fulfill the requirement of God's law completely, to its perfection, that is, to its completion.

Each curtain was four cubits wide. Therefore, the ten curtains were of the total width of ten times four cubits. These forty cubits covered the thirty cubit length of the tabernacle, leaving a ten cubit overhang at the rear, the west side. Ten and four signify that Christ, the righteous One, is the complete, perfect creature in full.

Besides all these numbers—two, four, five, seven, eight, and ten—there is also the number three. The curtains were twenty-eight cubits long, whereas the tabernacle was thirty cubits long and ten cubits wide. When the curtains were placed lengthwise across the top of the tabernacle, they covered the ten-cubit width on top, leaving nine cubits hanging on the north and south sides. This nine is composed of three times three.

The basic numbers of the curtains are three, four, five, and seven, because these are the basic numbers of God's building. Three represents the Triune God in resurrection, four represents the creatures, five represents man plus God to take responsibility, and seven represents perfection and completion. The dwelling place of God is man mingled with the Triune God. This dwelling place is built up by man in the Triune God bearing the full responsibility.

GOATS' HAIR

The second layer of the covering of the tabernacle was

made of goats' hair (Exo. 36:14). According to the parable in Matthew 25:31-46, the goat represents a sinful person. Furthermore, the hairs of the goat represent the sins coming out of the sinful person. Therefore, whereas the first layer represents Christ as our righteousness before God, the second layer represents Christ becoming sin for us (2 Cor. 5:21). He is the One who knew no sin but became sin for us. The first layer signifies Christ as the One who knew no sin, the righteous One and our righteousness before God, but the second layer signifies that in the eyes of God, when Christ was on the cross, He became sin for us.

Concerning the curtains of goats' hair, Exodus 36:16 says, "He joined five of the curtains by themselves, and six of the curtains by themselves." The layer of goats' hair is not composed of ten curtains but of eleven. Eleven is something more than ten but short of twelve. In the Scriptures ten is a positive figure, representing human completion. Twelve, in the Scriptures, is also positive, representing eternal perfection (Rev. 21:12, 14, 16). However, eleven, greater than ten and short of twelve, is not positive. A person with eleven fingers would appear wrong and abnormal. Eleven is something beyond that which was meant to be and indicates sinfulness. Sin is something extra which was not meant to be. The eleven curtains represent sin itself. Sin spoils the completion and the perfection of man before God.

With the layer of goats' hair, the numbers seven and eight cannot be found. You cannot derive seven, because the length of the curtains of goats' hair is thirty cubits instead of twenty-eight (Exo. 36:15). This indicates that there is no resurrection or completion due to the involvement of sin.

With the first layer of fine twined linen, there were fifty loops of blue on each joining of five curtains (vv. 11-12). Furthermore, these loops were joined by gold clasps (v. 13), representing the divine nature. The joining power for the building of God, the church, is the heavenliness and the divine nature of Christ. If we lose the heavenliness and the divine nature of Christ, we will automatically be separated, for there will be no joining power between us. The more we are in the heavenliness and the more we are in the divine nature of Christ, the more we are strengthened to be joined together. With the second layer of goats' hair, however, the clasps were made of bronze rather than of gold (v. 18). Bronze, in type, represents judgment, trial, and testing. Because the second layer signifies that Christ became sin to be judged by God, the joining power here is the ability to be judged, tested, and tried. The power to suffer the judgment, test, and trial of God and even the tests of Satan is the joining power of the second covering of the tabernacle.

RAMS' SKINS DYED RED

The third layer of the covering was made of rams' skins dyed red (v. 19a). A ram is a male, and the dyeing of red signifies the shedding of blood for redemption. The third layer signifies that Christ was slain on the cross, shedding His blood to redeem us from our sins.

PORPOISE SKINS

The last layer of the covering was porpoise skins, the protection and safeguard for the tabernacle (v. 19b). Christ, who is the righteousness of God, became sin in the eyes of God and died, shedding His blood to redeem us from our sins and becoming the protection and the safeguard of the church. From the inside, the tabernacle looks very beautiful and glorious. But from the outside, it appears very coarse. It is the same with the church. If people come into the church, they will see the beauty of Christ and the glories of Christ. But when viewed from the outside by the worldly people, the church seems worthless and coarse, like porpoise skins. However, this worthless looking layer is the enduring strength of the church to stand against all manner of attacks.

CHAPTER SEVEN

THE BOARDS AND PILLARS
OF THE TABERNACLE

Scripture Reading: Exo. 36:20-38

ACACIA WOOD OVERLAID WITH GOLD

Exodus 36 speaks of the building of the boards and the pillars of the tabernacle. The boards and pillars composed the main structures of the tabernacle. Although in principle the tabernacle is a type of Christ (John 1:14; 2:19-21), Christ is more fully typified by the Ark of the Testimony (Exo. 37:1-9). Because the tabernacle was built not with one board but with forty-eight boards joined together, it also signifies the church as the dwelling place of God, composed of many believers who have been joined together (Eph. 2:21-22). Strictly speaking, the Ark typifies Christ, and the tabernacle typifies the church.

The Ark was composed of acacia wood, signifying the human nature of Christ, overlaid with gold, signifying the divine nature of Christ. The boards of the tabernacle were also made of acacia wood overlaid with gold. Because the boards were constructed of the same two elements as the Ark, they are the enlargement, the expansion, of the Ark. The church, which is the Body of Christ, is the enlargement, the expansion, of Christ as the Head. The two natures of Christ, the human nature and the divine nature, are joined together and mingled as one. When this principle of mingling is enlarged, the church is produced. The church, in principle, is the same as Christ—the human nature is mingled with the divine nature to become one entity. The church is composed not only of God Himself, nor merely of human nature alone. It is an entity of two different natures mingled together and joined into one, as typified by the acacia wood overlaid with gold.

THE MEASUREMENTS OF THE BOARDS

The measurements of the boards are very significant. Exodus 36:21 says, "Ten cubits was the length of a board, and one and a half cubits, the width of each board." In principle, ten cubits may be divided into two sections, each consisting of five cubits, just as the Ten Commandments are divided into two groups of five each, and the ten curtains are divided into two sections joined together (vv. 8, 10). As we have seen before, five signifies the number of responsibility. Furthermore, two indicates a testimony (Matt. 18:16). Therefore, the length and the materials of the boards signify the responsibility for the testimony of God's building, taken by us who have been regenerated with the nature of God.

The width of the boards was one and a half cubits. Since the basic numbers of God's building are three and five, we may realize that one and a half is simply half of the number three. This signifies that one board is not complete in itself. It must be completed by another board. Two boards joined together complete the number three. This principle is quite clear in the Scriptures; in Luke 10:1-16 the Lord sent the disciples out by twos. As members of the church none of us should be individualistic. Individualism is against the principle of the Body, the house of God. By ourselves, individually, we can never be complete. We are merely half a unit. We all must be related together to be complete. In principle, we must go in pairs.

THE TENONS AND SOCKETS

Exodus 36:22a and 24 say, "Each board had two tenons joined to one another...And he made forty sockets of silver under the twenty boards, two sockets under one board for its two tenons and two sockets under the next board for its two tenons." Beneath each board there were two tenons. Here again is the number two, the number of testimony and confirmation. We need both the testimony and the confirmation. A testimony is given by us to others, and confirmation is something received by us from others. We must be confirmed by others. If one board were to have only one tenon, it would be easy for it to turn and even fall down. One board with two tenons is more stable, not easily turning or falling. Some brothers or sisters may easily be turned or changed. Last month they may have been doing quite well, but now they have changed and are no longer doing well. It seems that they have only one tenon instead of two. If we have two tenons, we will be stable. It will not be easy for us to have such a change or to fall because we are always confirmed by others and can give testimony to others.

With each tenon there was a socket made of silver (v. 24). Silver represents redemption. The redemption of the Lord is the base on which the building of God is laid. These silver sockets were very weighty. According to 38:27, each socket was of a talent of silver, the equivalent of about one hundred pounds. The tenons of the boards were placed into the sockets of silver. Forty-eight boards had two sockets each. Another four sockets were cast for the four pillars which bore the inner veil (36:36). This totaled to one hundred sockets of silver. One hundred in the Scriptures signifies fullness and completion. The Lord said that some would bear fruit thirtyfold, sixtyfold, and one hundredfold (Matt. 13:8), indicating fruit-bearing in fullness. The redemption of the Lord as the base of the tabernacle is in fullness. There is nothing short; Christ's redemption is absolutely full and complete.

THE NUMBER OF THE BOARDS

On the south side of the tabernacle there were twenty boards (Exo. 36:23), and on the north side there were twenty more (v. 25). There were two sets of twenty, again signifying a testimony. Furthermore, twenty itself is two times ten, signifying the testimony of completeness. Twenty may also be figured as four times five. Four is the number of the creatures in God's creation. Man as a created being takes up the responsibility to have a testimony by being regenerated, by having God added to him.

Exodus 36:27 through 29 say, "For the rear of the tabernacle westward he made six boards. And two boards he made for the corners of the tabernacle in the rear. And they were double below, and at its top they were completely joined to a single ring; thus he did to both of them for the two corners." At the rear of the tabernacle there were six boards, totaling nine cubits in width (v. 27). These may be divided into three pairs, each pair being three cubits wide. At the two corners of the west side there were another two boards (vv. 27-29). These two boards were made in a peculiar and special way. According to the Hebrew, verse 29 says that they were "doubled from below" for strength. According to the Scriptures, the corner is crucial for God's building (Matt. 21:42). The corner joins the two sides of the wall. It stands to meet all kinds of situations and to withstand all kinds of attacks. Therefore, the corners must be strengthened. In the church some are like the boards at the corner. If you took away such ones, the church would be weakened. The church could be joined together and stand strongly because of these "corner boards."

The six boards plus the two corner boards totaled to eight. Without the corner boards, the other boards would number to six. By itself, six does not have a positive connotation. The number six is the number of the created and unregenerated man, for man was made on the sixth day. With these two corner boards, however, the number comes to eight. Eight signifies resurrection. The strengthening power of the church is the resurrection power.

The total of all the boards of the tabernacle was forty-eight. Forty-eight is composed of six times eight. All the created men, typified by the boards, are now in resurrection. The boards signify men, who were created on the sixth day, but are now in Christ, that is, in resurrection. Their number has become eight.

THE BARS AND THE RINGS

Verses 31 through 34 speak of the bars for the boards of the tabernacle. The bars were made of the same material as the boards, that is, of acacia wood overlaid with gold. They signify the Holy Spirit as the uniting Spirit, who joins all the members of the Body into one (Eph. 4:3). The revelation of the

Spirit as acacia wood overlaid with gold is very deep. With the Spirit, there is the divine nature and there is also the human nature. The Spirit of God before the Lord's incarnation was different from the Spirit after the Lord's incarnation. Before the Lord's incarnation, the Spirit was mainly the Spirit of God (Gen. 1:2). With the Spirit of God, there was only the divine nature. But after the incarnation, the resurrection, and the ascension of Christ, the Holy Spirit, the Spirit of God, is now the Spirit of Christ (Rom. 8:9). Christ has not only the divine nature but also the human nature. Therefore, the Spirit of this Christ is the Spirit with two natures, the divine nature and the human nature mingled together.

John 7:38-39 says, "He who believes into Me, as the Scripture said, out of his innermost being shall flow rivers of living water. But this He said concerning the Spirit, whom those who believed into Him were about to receive; for the Spirit was not yet, because Jesus had not yet been glorified." At the time the Lord spoke this verse, the Spirit had not yet come. On the one hand, the Spirit in the Old Testament had come already. Many times the Spirit of Jehovah came to visit people (Judg. 6:34; 14:5-6, 19; 1 Sam. 11:6; 16:13; 2 Chron. 24:20). But the Spirit of Christ, at the time when the Lord Jesus spoke this word, had not yet come. The Spirit of Jehovah was the Spirit with the divine nature but without the human nature. But after the resurrection the Spirit of Christ comes with two natures, the divine nature and the human nature. As a type of the Spirit, the bars in the tabernacle were of two materials, wood overlaid with gold.

Exodus 36:31 and 32 say that the bars were divided into three groups of five, one on the south side, one on the north side, and one on the rear side. Verse 33 goes on to say, "He made the middle bar to pass through in the center of the boards from end to end." By these three verses we may infer that there were five bars in three lines on each side. On each side, the middle bar reached from end to end in one line. The lines of bars above and below the middle bar each were made of two bars, two pieces. Two bars formed the first line, one bar from end to end was the second line, and two bars formed the last line. Three lines were composed of five bars. The middle

bar was twice the length of the other bars, providing balance.
If the middle bar had been in two pieces, there would have
been a weakness at the center of the wall, and the two halves
of each side would have been without balance.

Here again are the numbers three and five, with the three
groups of five bars signifying the Spirit of the Triune God to
take the responsibility for God's building. The Holy Spirit, the
Spirit of Christ, the Spirit with the two natures—the divine
nature and the human nature—bears the responsibility for
God's building.

Verse 34 says, "He overlaid the boards with gold and made
their rings of gold as holders for the bars, and overlaid the
bars with gold." The golden rings represent the joining strength
of the Holy Spirit (Eph. 4:3). The forty-eight boards were
joined together not by themselves but absolutely by the gold.
If the gold were to be removed from the forty-eight standing
boards, they would all be separated from each other. They
were joined together in the gold. Each board was overlaid
with gold, on the gold there were the golden rings, and within
the golden rings there were the golden bars. The oneness of
all the believers in the Body is in the divine nature. If we are
not living in the divine nature and life of Christ, we are separated from one another. We can be one only in Christ, in the
divine nature and in the divine life. Without the gold, the
boards would have been separated from each other, but in the
gold they were joined together.

THE PILLARS, THE VEIL, AND THE SCREEN

Exodus 36:35-38 speaks concerning the pillars in the
tabernacle which supported the veil and the screen. The inner
veil separated the Holy of Holies from the Holy Place. The
screen, or the outer veil, on the other hand, was at the
entrance of the tabernacle separating the outer court from
the Holy Place. The veil was upon four pillars, made with
the same materials as the boards and the bars, acacia wood
overlaid with gold, and were based on four silver sockets.
The screen was upon five pillars of acacia wood overlaid with
gold, but it was based on bronze sockets. The inner entrance
to God's building is based on the redemption which Christ

accomplished, and the judgments, trials, tests, and temptations suffered by Christ form the base of the outer entrance.

At the screen there were four entrances formed by five pillars. Four refers to man as the leading one of the creatures. The entrance of the tabernacle, the dwelling place and building of God, is toward man. All men as redeemed creatures may enter in through this entrance. At the veil, the inner entrance, four pillars formed three entrances. The inner entrance represents the Triune God, signified by the number three. By passing through the screen and the veil, the creatures come into the Triune God. The numbers four and three may be added to form seven. They may also be multiplied to form twelve. These two numbers, seven and twelve, are the main numbers of the book of Revelation. In chapter 1 of Revelation there are the seven churches (vv. 12, 20), and in chapter 21 there is the number twelve, the number of the New Jerusalem (vv. 12-21). Those who enter the tabernacle are according to the number seven, but in the New Jerusalem they will be according to the number twelve.

The first entrance into the tabernacle is characterized by the number four, and the second entrance, by the number three. The building of God is open to man as a redeemed creature. When he comes into the tabernacle, he meets the three inner entrances, signifying the Triune God, so that he may enter into the Triune God.

Upon the inner veil were sown the cherubim (Exo. 36:35), signifying the glory of God (Heb. 9:5). However, the screen did not have the cherubim. The glory of God within the church is always concealed. It is something inward, not outward. The glory of God with His people is always concealed and can be seen only from within God's building.

CHAPTER EIGHT

THE EIGHTFOLD SIGNIFICANCE
OF THE TABERNACLE

Scripture Reading: Exo. 36:31-38; 37:1-9; Gal. 2:9; Rev. 3:12; John 10:9

In this chapter we will review eight points related to the tabernacle so that we may be more deeply impressed with them. These eight matters are basic for the building up of the church.

THE REDEMPTION OF CHRIST

We have seen that the church is built on the basis of the redemption of Christ, as typified by the one hundred silver sockets (Exo. 36:24, 26, 30, 36). The whole tabernacle was grounded on the silver sockets. The base and foundation of the silver sockets is one of the most significant aspects of the tabernacle. Exodus 38:27 tells us that the sockets were very large and heavy, each being of one talent, the equivalent of almost one hundred pounds. The heaviest part of the tabernacle was the foundation. The tabernacle was not grounded on the earth. It was based and grounded on the silver sockets. It was something different from the earth and separated from the earth. This shows us that the church is not grounded or built upon something of the earth but on something apart from the earth, the full and weighty redemption of Christ. One hundred, the number of the silver sockets, indicates that there is nothing short in Christ's redemption. It is absolutely complete, full, and weighty. It is the foundation of the church and the basis for the building of the Lord's dwelling place.

THE MANIFESTATION OF THE DIVINE NATURE

The foundation of the tabernacle was of silver, but the manifestation within the tabernacle was the gold (36:13, 34, 36, 38; 37:1-28). From within the tabernacle, one could see almost nothing but gold. Gold signifies the divine nature with the divine life of Christ, which is God Himself. The church is built upon the foundation of the redemption of Christ, but what the church manifests is the divine nature and divine life of Christ. Within the church, the building of God, what must be manifested is not the works, the doings of God, but the very nature and life of God. The manifestation of the divine nature is more significant than even the foundation of the tabernacle. The tabernacle was full of gold, and the church must be full of the divine nature of God. What we manifest, express, and show to others should be nothing other than the glorious divine nature of Christ.

THE TRANSFORMED HUMAN NATURE

What is manifested in the church is the divine nature, but the manifestation of the divine nature depends upon the human nature. The gold of the tabernacle overlaid the acacia wood (36:20, 31, 36; 37:1, 4). What was manifested was the gold, but the gold overlaid the acacia wood. In a sense, the gold depended upon the acacia wood. This may seem strange to our concept. We may have thought that the condition of our human nature depends upon the divine nature. But the picture of the tabernacle shows that the gold depends upon the wood.

With the building of the church, the divine nature of God depends greatly upon our human nature. The gold did not stand upright in the tabernacle; it was the acacia wood which stood with the gold upon it (36:20). Gold is a soft metal and is not hard enough to stand upright. The standing strength for the tabernacle was not with the gold but with the acacia wood. Without the acacia wood, the gold could not stand.

As we have seen, the acacia wood represents the transformed human nature and character. According to the history of the church, the building of the church has depended very much upon the transformed human nature. Brothers such as

Martin Luther, George Müller, and John Darby had a transformed human nature, and their character was strong. If you
would read their biographies, you could see that they were
the real acacia wood. The building of the church needs the
proper human character. The manifestation in the church is
the divine nature with the divine life, but the support is the
human character, the human nature. The standing strength
needed for the tabernacle is with the human nature "overlaid," that is, transformed, with the divine nature and divine
life of Christ. The human nature and the divine nature must
be mingled together.

THE TWO TENONS FOR BALANCE

The fourth point with which we must be deeply impressed
is related to the two tenons under each board (v. 22). There
are always two sides, two aspects, to the things created by
God. As a member in the church you are one board, but you
must have two tenons. The two tenons may be compared to
your two feet. You are one person but with two feet. Your feet
are needed for balance. If you stand upon one foot, you will
eventually lose your balance. We must always be balanced
by the number two. Not only do we have two feet, but we
also have two hands, two arms, two shoulders, and even two
ears and two eyes. Everything is in twos for balance. We must
remember that we always have to be balanced by others. If
anything stands alone, it will lose its balance. We must always
be checked, tested, and confirmed by others that we may have
the balance. Otherwise, we will be peculiar and will go to an
extreme. The significance of the two tenons is that they show
us our need for balance.

As we have seen before, if a board had only one tenon, it
would turn easily and even fall, just as we may easily fall if
we stand on one foot. When we are walking and wish to turn,
we must lift one foot off the ground. We cannot turn when we
are standing on two feet. Many Christians today may easily be
turned. They are like a board with one tenon. Spiritually speaking, they may face in one direction today, but tomorrow they
may face in the opposite direction. It is easy for such ones to
be changed and fall because they do not have two tenons.

BEING COMPLETED
FOR THE BUILDING OF THE CHURCH

The width of the boards of the tabernacle was one and a half cubits (v. 21), indicating a half measurement of three cubits. One half always needs the other half. As members of the Body, we are just one half. We must remember that we always need another member to make us complete. In creation there is the same principle. A man is not complete unless he has a wife. Likewise, a woman is not complete unless she is married to a husband. The couple is the completion. The husband is one half, and the wife is another half. Sometimes when the brothers and sisters come into the meeting, a wife and her husband may sit together as one whole. Each is a half, and they both need the other half to make them a whole. For the building of the church, our need is to be completed. We can never be individuals; we must always be completed by others.

JOINED BY THE HOLY SPIRIT

We must be joined with others by the Holy Spirit and in the Holy Spirit with the holding power of the divine nature. According to 36:31-34, the bars of acacia wood overlaid with gold were in the golden rings, and the golden rings were joined to the gold overlaying the boards. This typifies the holding strength and the holding power of the divine nature and life of Christ. All the boards were joined together within the gold and by the bars overlaid with gold. The boards could be joined together as one simply because they were in the gold; that is, in type, they were in the divine nature and divine life of Christ.

The strength and the power for joining together was the bars, which represent the Holy Spirit. According to 36:31 and 32, there were five bars on the south side, five bars on the north side, and five bars on the west side. The three groups of bars indicate that this Spirit is the Spirit of the Triune God.

We must be impressed with the picture in Exodus 36. There were three groups of bars, and each group consisted of five bars. Five is four plus one. As we have seen, four bars were smaller and one bar, the middle one, was bigger, extending from one end of a wall to the other end. This is a picture of the mingling of the divine nature with the human nature. Four represents the creature, and one represents the Creator. These two added together become five. Moreover, five signifies responsibility. Therefore, the bars signify the Holy Spirit of the Triune God, who takes the full responsibility for God's building by mingling His divine nature with the human nature. How could the church be built up with so many believers? It could be done only in the divine nature and divine life of Christ by the Spirit of the Triune God.

COVERED BY A FOURFOLD CHRIST

The entire tabernacle was covered by a fourfold covering, which represents the fourfold Christ (vv. 8-19). The tabernacle was grounded on the silver sockets and was covered with the fourfold covering. This means that even though the church is grounded on the redemption of Christ, it still has to be covered by Christ, not by a simple Christ but by a fourfold Christ. The first layer of the coverings was made of linen. This is something of the vegetable life. The second layer was made of goats' hair, the third layer was of rams' skins, and the last layer was made of porpoise skins, all something of the animal life. The goats' hair and the rams' skins were of the life of the animals belonging to the flock on the land, but the porpoise skins were from the animals of the sea. The picture of the coverings shows us that with Christ there are different aspects of life. There is an aspect of life pictured by linen, and there is the aspect of life pictured by the rams and the goats. There is also another aspect of life pictured by the porpoise in the sea.

The Lord in His human life is perfect, as represented by the white linen. Furthermore, this Christ bears the heavenly character, the kingship, the authority of heaven, the redemption, and even the glory of God, as signified by the blue, the purple, the scarlet, and the cherubim of the linen curtains.

The significance of the goats' hair and the rams' skins is related to redemption. Flocks of rams and goats are not good for protection. They are good only for sacrifice. Christ has the life that would sacrifice for others, the life that would die, shedding His blood to accomplish redemption, as signified by the rams' skins dyed red. This is another aspect of the life of Christ.

The life of the porpoise in the sea represents the life which is strong enough to endure all kinds of trials and to suffer all kinds of tests, temptations, and the attacks of death. Sea water represents the power of death. Even under the power of death, that is, under the sea water, the porpoise can live and withstand pressure. Even under the attacks of death, such a Christ is still able to live.

The Christ depicted by the coverings of the tabernacle is not a simple Christ but a manifold Christ, a Christ of many aspects. The church must experience this Christ so that we may be covered by Him.

THE NEED FOR THE PILLARS

In the previous chapter we have seen that there were nine pillars in the tabernacle (vv. 36, 38). At the entrance to the tabernacle five pillars supported the screen, and at the entrance to the Holy of Holies four pillars supported the veil. In the church there are some who are the pillars. Galatians 2:9 says, "Perceiving the grace given to me, James and Cephas and John, who were reputed to be pillars." Peter, James, and John, as the mature and stronger ones, were not merely boards but the pillars of the church. Similarly, in Revelation 3:12 the Lord promised the church in Philadelphia that "he who overcomes, him I will make a pillar in the temple of My God."

The pillars are different from the boards. The boards which form the wall of the tabernacle are good for protection and separation, but there is no way for people to enter into God's building through them. The pillars, on the other hand, are good for both protection and separation as well as for entrance. For this reason, to be a pillar, one must be much stronger than the boards.

The boards are useful for protection, sanctification, holiness, and for separation from the world. They are strong to stand against all the negative things. Praise the Lord that we have so many brothers and sisters who exclude the negative things. Without them, there would be no wall. The church would be too open and exposed to the negative things. There would be no protection and no building up of the dwelling place of God. For the building, we need brothers and sisters to be the separating boards. The separating boards are like the wall of the New Jerusalem (21:12), separating and protecting by life.

However, if we are all boards, then there will be no entrance for people to come into God's dwelling place. The church will be closed, and we will become exclusive. For the sake of the entrance, some of us have to be dealt with. A pillar is finer and stronger than a board. The boards must be cut and fitted to become the pillars. On the one hand, to be cut and fitted is to be reduced, but on the other hand, it is to be increased in strength. Those who have been dealt with will be very flexible. They can be for protection and support, and they can also be the entrance for others to come into God's dwelling place. People will be free to go in through them.

We pray that the Lord would increase the numbers in the churches, but for this there is the need for some among the believers to become the pillars. The number of the boards was forty-eight, but the number of the pillars was only nine. The majority are the boards, whereas the minority are the pillars. We need the pillars to bring in the liberty of the Holy Spirit, to provide the entrance for men as redeemed creatures to come into the Triune God.

In John 10:9 the Lord said, "I am the door; if anyone enters through Me, he shall be saved and shall go in and go out and shall find pasture." The sheep may go in and go out through Him. They have the liberty through the Lord as the entrance for coming in and going out. With the church there is the need of the separating wall, and there is the need of the entrances for people to come into the Triune God with full liberty.

The first entrance was of five pillars, signifying responsibility. The second entrance was of four pillars, pointing to man, the creature. In total there were nine pillars, which is three times three. This indicates something threefold in the Triune God. The pillars are in the Triune God to a threefold degree to take up the responsibility to form the entrances for the men as redeemed creatures to come into the Triune God.

CHAPTER NINE

THE CONTENTS OF THE TABERNACLE

(1)

Scripture Reading: Exo. 37:10-29

THREE ASPECTS OF CHRIST

Chapter 37 of Exodus is a record of the building of the contents of the tabernacle. The table of the bread of the Presence, the lampstand, and the incense altar were the contents of the Holy Place. These three items formed one category of the contents of the tabernacle, and the other category was a single item, the Ark in the Holy of Holies. In this chapter and in the next, we will present the main features, the most significant characteristics, of these items.

The three items of the first group reveal to us three aspects of Christ for our experience and for the Father's pleasure. In 37:10-29 the table of the bread of the Presence is mentioned first, followed by the lampstand, and then the altar. The bread set forth upon the table was the bread of the Presence (25:30), referring to the presence of God. The table of the bread of the Presence represents Christ as our life supply (John 6:33-35, 51), the lampstand represents Christ as our light (1:4; 8:12), and the altar of incense represents Christ as the sweet savor for us toward God (Eph. 5:2). John 1:4 says, "In Him was life, and the life was the light of men." This verse corresponds to the order of our experience of Christ. We experience Christ first as life, and then this life is the light to us. The issue, the result, of our experience of life and light is Christ as the sweet savor to God for us. When we truly experience Christ as life to us, we are in the light of life, and when we are in the light of life, we share and experience Christ as the sweet savor to God. We become acceptable to God through Him and in Him as the sweet savor. He is the means by which and in which we are pleasing to God.

Life, light, and the sweet savor of the incense as aspects of Christ are significant and very full of meaning. The number of these items is three, the number of the Triune God. At the table, God the Son is our life; at the lampstand, God the Spirit is our light; and at the incense altar, God the Father is pleased with the sweet savor of Christ. These three items are very different from our own works, our own knowledge, and our own morality. We may be walking, working, and doing things according to our own knowledge and our own morality. We must be clear that such a work and walk are versus Christ. Our work is versus Christ as life, our knowledge are versus Christ as light, and our morality is versus the sweet savor of Christ. If we are going to enjoy Christ as life, as light, and as the sweet savor, we have to deny our own work, knowledge, and morality. If we depend upon our own work, we will not enjoy Christ as life. If we walk and work according to our knowledge, we could never enjoy and experience Christ as our light. Moreover, if we take our own morality for our acceptance to God, then we could not experience Christ as our sweet savor toward God. To deny and reject our own work, knowledge, and morality is to reject our whole self. There is no place for ourselves. There is only place for Christ—Christ as our life, Christ as our light, and Christ as our sweet savor to God. Everything must be Christ.

THE STANDARD OF THE TABLE
OF THE BREAD OF THE PRESENCE

Exodus 37:10 says, "He made the table of acacia wood: two cubits was its length, and a cubit its width, and one and a half cubits its height." The height of the table is the same as that of the Ark of the Testimony in verse 1. This indicates that the Lord comes up to the standard of the testimony of God so that He could be life to us. If He were short of the testimony of God, He would not be able to be life to us.

The table was one cubit wide and two cubits long, forming

two square cubits. Because one square cubit represents a complete unit, the length and width of the table constitute two complete units, representing the testimony of Christ being life to us. Our experience always testifies that Christ is life. By experiencing Him, we could testify that Christ is truly life to us.

THE WEIGHT OF THE LAMPSTAND

No measurement is given for the size of the lampstand, signifying that there is no measurement for the light. The light in the Holy Spirit is immeasurable. You may say, "I saw a great light" (Matt. 4:16), but you cannot say how great the light was. There is no measurement for the light, but there is a weight to the light. Exodus 37:24 says that the lampstand and its utensils were made of one talent of gold, which is close to one hundred pounds. With Christ as light to us there is no measurement, but there is always the weight. The more we are in the light of Christ, the more we experience Christ as the light, the weightier we are. We know this by our experience. When we are in darkness, we are a very light person. But when we are in the light of Christ, we become a man of weight. On the one hand, we may refer to someone as a man of weight, a weighty person. On the other hand, we may say of another person that he is too light. To be too light simply means to be too much in darkness. The more we are in darkness, the lighter we are. No one in darkness is weighty. But the more we are in the light of Christ, the weightier we are. We become men of weight. There is no measurement to the lampstand, but there is the weight.

THE TESTIMONY OF THE TABLE
AND THE INCENSE ALTAR

Verse 25 says, "He made the altar of incense of acacia wood; a cubit was its length, and a cubit, its width, square; and two cubits, its height." The incense altar was one cubit square and two cubits high. This is two units of a cube. One cubit wide, one cubit long, and one cubit high forms a perfect cube, a perfect and complete whole. Nothing can be added and nothing can be subtracted from it. Christ is so perfect and complete, just like a cube. He is so acceptable and pleasing to God because He is so perfect and complete. You can never add anything to Him, and you can never take away anything from Him. The height of the incense altar being a cube doubled indicates that the incense altar is a testimony before God.

The altar of incense is a testimony before God, whereas the table of the bread of the Presence is a testimony toward us. The table was two cubits long and one cubit wide (v. 10), constituting two units of one square cubit each, placed next to each other horizontally. The altar, on the other hand, was of two cubes placed vertically. Both the table and the altar were two cubits by one, but the table was doubled horizontally as a testimony to us, whereas the altar was doubled vertically as a testimony to God. What Christ is as a testimony to us horizontally comes up to the standard of what Christ is as the testimony to God vertically. The length of the table is the same as the height of the altar. Both the table and the altar signify the one Christ. When He comes to you as the table, He is horizontal, but when He goes to God as the incense, He is vertical.

A TESTIMONY OF COORDINATION

Exodus 37:3-5 tells us that there were four rings in the Ark through which poles were placed so that it could be carried by four men. According to verses 13 through 15 there were also four rings in the table of the bread of the Presence. Furthermore, verse 27 says that two rings were placed under the rim of the altar for the same purpose. The Ark and the table probably required four people to carry them. However, it may have been that only two persons were required to carry the altar, since both its length and width were one cubit. The two poles in two rings could have been borne upon one man's two shoulders at either end. Nevertheless, the Ark and the table required at least four men to carry them. This points to the coordination of the Body of Christ. On one side of the Ark and the table were two rings, indicating a testimony. A pole was placed through the two rings, and two men formed a group to bear the one side. Another pole was on the other side within the two other rings, and another two men bore that side. These two groups formed one group of four. This signifies the coordination of the creatures to bear the testimony. The four men had to be nearly the same size. One could not be too tall or too short, lest they not be able to coordinate. They had to coordinate and walk together in the same steps (2 Cor. 12:18b).

The table and, in principle, the incense altar were borne in the same way as the Ark. Second Samuel 6 and 1 Chronicles 13 record how David brought the Ark to Jerusalem, not borne by men but upon a new cart. That displeased the Lord, and His anger was kindled (2 Sam. 6:7). From this, David learned a lesson. The next time the Ark was moved, David realized that the divine way to carry the Ark was not by a cart but upon the shoulders of the Levites (1 Chron. 15:2, 13-15) for the testimony of the Body.

CHRIST AS LIGHT IN RESURRECTION

Although there is no measurement for the lampstand, there are many occurrences of the number three in the description of the lampstand. Exodus 37:18 says, "There were six branches going out of its sides; three branches of the lampstand out of one of its sides, and three branches of the lampstand out of its other side." The lampstand had six branches, three on two sides. Three, here, represents resurrection, and two represents a testimony. On each branch there were three cups shaped like almond blossoms with calyxes and blossoming buds (v. 19). The calyx is the leafy green layer of a flower, and the blossoming bud is the flower itself. The word *cup* is used to describe the whole flower, including the calyx and the blossoming bud. In addition to a calyx and the blossoming bud, an almond blossom also has the almond fruit. The whole flower, including calyx and blossom, was a cup to bear the oil for lighting.

According to Numbers 17:8, Aaron's rod budded, blossomed, and bore almonds. This is a picture of resurrection, life coming out of death. Aaron's rod was a dead stick, but through resurrection it brought forth almonds. The almond blossoms with the calyxes and blossoming buds depict the issue of the resurrection life of Christ. Christ as light to us is the issue of Christ as life to us. The resurrection life of Christ is for the light. Christ could be light to us by passing through resurrection.

The lampstand is full of symbols of resurrection. Every branch of the lampstand is like a branch of an almond tree. Furthermore, the many occurrences of groups of three on the lampstand indicate resurrection. On each branch of the lampstand were three almond blossoms with a calyx and blossoming bud. When the flower blossoms, it yields the almond as fruit. This indicates that the resurrection life is the light to us.

Exodus 37:20-21 says, "On the lampstand were four cups made like almond blossoms, its calyxes and its blossom buds; and a calyx under two branches of one piece with it, and a calyx under two branches of one piece with it, and a calyx under two branches of one piece with it, for the six branches going out of it." There were six branches, and at the base where each pair of branches met there was a calyx. On each of the six branches there were three calyxes. Three branches were on one side, and three branches were on the other side. At the base of three pairs of branches there were three calyxes, and on each branch there were three almond blossoms. This totaled to seven groups of three blossoms.

On the shaft of the lampstand there were an additional four almond blossoms (v. 20). It is very meaningful that there is at least one mention of the number four in the lampstand. If there had been no number four, the lampstand may have had nothing to do with us as the creatures. Thus, with the lampstand there are the number three and the number six, and with the stalk of the lampstand there is the number four. The basic number is three, signifying that the entire lampstand is a matter of resurrection. But this resurrection is for man, the creature, because Christ as light is a man, that is, a creature, as signified by the four almond blossoms on the stalk. If He were not a creature, He would be the light, but He would not be light to us. Because He is a creature, He is light to man, who is signified by the number six, since man was created on the sixth day. The light of Christ is wholly a matter in resurrection. Christ is life and light in resurrection, but He is also a creature that He may be light to man. More-over, verse 24 says that the lampstand was of a talent of gold, signifying the divine nature. The light of the lampstand is the divine light of the divine nature.

CHAPTER TEN

THE CONTENTS OF THE TABERNACLE

(2)

Scripture Reading: Exo. 37:1-9

Chapter 37 of Exodus speaks concerning the contents of the tabernacle. The tabernacle was the dwelling place, the house, of the Lord. Within every house, every dwelling place, there must be some contents. Within the tabernacle there were four main items as the contents. The first item was the Ark (vv. 1-9), the second item was the table of the bread of the Presence (vv. 10-16), the third item was the lampstand (vv. 17-24), and the fourth item was the altar of incense (vv. 25-28). The tabernacle was divided into two parts—the inner part and the outer part. The inner part was the Holy of Holies, and the outer part was the Holy Place. Accordingly, these four main items as the contents of the tabernacle were divided into two groups. One group was of one item, and the other group was of three items. Within the inner part, the Holy of Holies, there was only the Ark as its content. Within the outer part, the Holy Place, there were three items—the table, the lampstand, and the incense altar—as its contents. These four items as the contents of the tabernacle are full of deep meaning. In this chapter we will fellowship concerning the Ark of the Testimony.

THE ARK OF THE TESTIMONY

The Ark was called the Ark of the Testimony of God (Exo. 39:35; 40:3, 5, 21). Within the Ark there were the two tablets of the Ten Commandments. The Ten Commandments are the definition, the description, the explanation, of God. Most people consider that the Ten Commandments are merely ten laws set up by God for us to keep. This concept is not correct. The Ten Commandments are actually a full definition of God, showing us what kind of God He is. A law is always an explanation of the one who makes it. A person will make a law according to what he is. If you are a good person, you will make good laws. If you are an evil person, you will spontaneously make evil laws. Whatever one sets up as a law will be the definition, the explanation, of that person. The Ten Commandments given by God are a definition, an explanation, of God Himself. The Ten Commandments mainly show us that God is a God of holiness, a God of righteousness, a God of love, and a God of light.

The testimony of God is actually a person, who is the embodiment of God. The testimony was not only the Ten Commandments by themselves. Rather, it was the Ten Commandments within the Ark. This Ark was composed of two materials, acacia wood overlaid with gold, typifying Christ as the One with the human nature and divine nature mingled together. He is the One who is God Himself and was incarnated to be a man. The human nature and the divine nature were mingled and joined together to become one living person. Within this one living person is the law of God, that is, the definition, the explanation, of God. Christ is the testimony of God, a person who is the embodiment of what God is.

Exodus 37:1 speaks of the dimensions of the Ark: "Bezalel made the Ark of acacia wood: two and a half cubits was its length; and one and a half cubits, its width; and one and a half cubits, its height." All the dimensions of the Ark were half measurements. The length was two and a half cubits, the width was one and a half cubits, and the height was one and a half cubits. Two and a half is half of five, and one and a half is half of three. As we have seen before, three and five are the basic numbers in the building of God's dwelling place. Three signifies the Triune God, and five signifies the creature plus the Creator to bear the responsibility for God's building. The dimensions of the Ark are half of the basic numbers, signifying that the Ark is a testimony. A half implies that another half is needed for a full testimony. Half a watermelon causes us to realize that another half is needed for a whole melon. Furthermore, in married life we sometimes speak of a wife being her husband's other half. Thus, the husband and wife together make a complete unit. The fact that two and a half cubits is half of five and that one and a half cubits is half of three indicates that the Ark is a testimony. The halves imply another half, and these halves put together make up the testimony. The half dimensions of the Ark show us in figure that it is the testimony of God.

ACACIA WOOD OVERLAID WITH GOLD

Exodus 37:2 says of the Ark, "He overlaid it with pure gold inside and outside, and made a rim of gold around it." Christ not only manifests God Himself outwardly, but what is within Christ is also God Himself. Both what Christ manifested without and what Christ is within are God Himself. God dwells within Christ and fills Him. At the same time God is manifested upon Christ. Christ is filled with God within, and Christ is "overlaid" with God without.

However, the form of the Ark was not of the gold. The form, the shape, of the Ark was of the acacia wood. The wood formed the shape of the Ark. The manifestation was the gold, but the form was the wood. In the Gospel of John we may see both the form of Christ and the manifestation of Christ. The form of Christ in this Gospel is of a real man, signified by the acacia wood. As a man He was thirsty; He came to a woman, asking for a drink of water (4:7). As a man He was wearied on His journey (v. 6). Once He wept (11:35), and once He washed others' feet (13:5). He was altogether in the form of a man. He has the form of the acacia wood.

However, in the Gospel of John the manifestation of Christ is not of a man. The manifestation of Christ is God. He was God manifested in the flesh (1 Tim. 3:16). As a real man, in the form of a man, He came to a woman, asking for a drink of water, but the manifestation of this man and the content of this man were something not merely human. Someone very unique came to that woman that day. This very Someone was God manifested. On the one hand, He was in the form of a man, but on the other hand, He was the manifestation of God.

He was filled with God. He is the Ark made of acacia wood and overlaid inside and outside with gold. He is the unique One, the wonderful One, with the real form of real humanity but as the manifestation of God and with the content of God. What He is filled with is God Himself, and what He manifests is God Himself yet in the form of a man. The form of the Ark was of the wood but the appearance and the content of the Ark were of gold.

The Ark was the unique content of the Holy of Holies. The Holy of Holies was ten cubits long, ten cubits wide, and ten cubits high (Exo. 36:9-15; cf. 1 Kings 6:20). It was a cube of ten cubits. This means in type that it is something altogether perfect. Within this perfect place there was the Ark as the testimony of God. This testimony is a living person as the embodiment of all that God is. This living person is composed and constituted with the human nature as His form and with the divine nature as His content and manifestation. Within Christ as the testimony of God are the very constituents of God, represented by the Ten Commandments of the law, and upon Him is the appearance of God.

THE COVER OF THE ARK

Exodus 37:6-9 tells us that upon the Ark there was a cover which was called the mercy seat, the expiation cover. It was the cover, but it was also a seat. This seat, this cover, was the very spot where man could meet God, and God could meet man. God and man met together at this seat as the cover of the Ark.

If the Ark were uncovered and one were to come into the Holy of Holies, that is, into the very presence of God, he would immediately find the Ten Commandments which would show him where he was and testify what he was. He would find the commandment, "Honor your father and your mother" (20:12). This commandment would right away testify what he was. He may immediately be condemned by this commandment because he may not have been one who honored his parents. The open Ark would condemn him.

However, what is depicted in these verses is not an open Ark. All the commandments were covered by the expiation cover, and this cover became the seat where God could meet man, and man could meet God. The blood of the sin offering was brought into the Holy of Holies to be sprinkled on the expiation cover (Lev. 16:14, 15). Without the covering and without the shedding of blood to redeem us from our sins, the testimony of God, which is Christ Himself to testify what God is and to show us what we are, would be a condemnation to us. But, praise the Lord, there is a covering, there is a redemption. He died on the cross, shedding His blood to redeem us and to provide a cover. By this cover we could meet God, and God could meet us, with all the problems between man and God having been resolved. With this cover, with this seat of mercy, there is the reconciliation between God and man.

Upon the expiation cover there were two cherubim (Exo. 37:7-9), signifying the glory of God (Heb. 9:5). The glory of God is the manifestation of God. God manifested is glory. We may compare glory to the shining of electrical lights, which is the glory of the electricity. When God shines Himself out, He becomes the glory. God is manifested in Christ, so upon Christ you can see the glory of God.

The two cherubim signify the glory of God, that is, the manifestation of God. This manifestation, this glory of God, is the testimony. Exodus 37 tells us that there was not only one cherub but two cherubim. Two is the number of testimony. The glory of God becomes the testimony of God, and the testimony of God becomes the glory of God. Upon Christ and with Christ, there is the manifestation of God which is the glory of God, and this manifestation as the glory of God is the testimony of God. This truth is very rich and very deep in thought and meaning.

THE THREE REQUIREMENTS OF THE ARK

With the Ark there are three requirements which must be fulfilled in order that we may meet with God. The first requirement is the glory of God. If one would come into the Holy of Holies, he would immediately see the two cherubim, representing the glory of God. The second requirement is the holiness of God, signified by the gold. The cherubim were made of gold. The Ark was covered with the golden expiation

cover, and the Ark itself was overlaid with gold. Gold represents the holy nature of God. If one looked into the Ark, he
would see the Ten Commandments. The Ten Commandments
represent what God is, and they become the requirement of
God toward us. The requirements of the Ten Commandments
are simply the righteousness of God.

The glory of God, the holiness of God, and the righteousness of God become the requirements which must be fulfilled
before we can meet with God. Without meeting these three
requirements, we could never meet God and stand before
Him. Rather, we would die before Him. God is a God of glory, a
God of holiness, and a God of righteousness. At the Ark, the
two cherubim require something of us, the golden nature
requires something of us, and the Ten Commandments require
something of us.

Praise the Lord, upon the Ark was also the expiation cover,
upon which the redeeming blood was sprinkled. This settles
all problems and meets all the requirements. The seat of God,
in principle, is a seat of judgment (Rev. 20:11-12). But at the
Ark the seat of judgment becomes a seat of mercy. Without
the shedding of blood, the Lord Himself as the testimony of
God—with the glory of God, the holiness of God, and the
righteousness of God—could only be a judgment seat to us.
But because of the shedding of His redeeming blood, His
redemption for us, He became an expiation cover to us. Therefore, at the expiation cover, by His redemption through the
shedding of His blood, we can meet God, we can fellowship
with God, we can come into contact with God, and we can
even become one with God.

CHAPTER ELEVEN

THE TABERNACLE
OF THE TESTIMONY OF GOD

Scripture Reading: Exo. 38:21-31

Exodus 38:21 says, "This is the sum of the things for the tabernacle, the Tabernacle of Testimony." The tabernacle is called the Tabernacle of Testimony. As we have seen, the Ark is the Ark of Testimony (40:3). The purpose of the Ark was to be the testimony of God. The purpose of the tabernacle is the same in principle; it is also for the testimony of God. The tabernacle is the enlargement of the Ark. In size there was a difference, but in principle and in nature the tabernacle was the same as the Ark. The purpose of the church is to express God in the same way that Christ expresses God. In this respect, the church in principle and in nature is exactly the same as Christ. Christ is the testimony of God, and the church is also the testimony of God in Christ. The church is the increase of Christ, the enlargement of Christ. The Ark is the Ark of Testimony, and the tabernacle is also the Tabernacle of the Testimony of God.

The Ark could be the testimony of God because of its contents. The contents of the Ark were primarily the two tablets of the Ten Commandments, the law. The law with the commandments is the testimony, the definition, the explanation, and the expression of God. Without the law, the Ark could not have been the testimony of God, because without the law, there is no definition, or explanation, of God. The Ark could be the testimony of God because the explanation, the definition, of God was within it. Christ is the testimony of God because with Him there is the definition, the explanation, and the expression of God.

In the same principle, the tabernacle was the testimony of God because of its contents. The contents of the tabernacle were first the Ark, then the three items in the Holy Place: the table of the bread of the Presence, the lampstand, and the incense altar. With these contents the tabernacle was equipped and qualified to be the testimony of God in Christ. Without them the tabernacle would be empty and could never be the testimony.

The reason that the church could be the testimony of God in Christ is because the church is full of Christ as the Ark, the incense altar, the table of the bread of the Presence, and the lampstand. Because the church is full of Christ as all these items, it is the testimony of God in Christ. Exodus 37 mentions these items as the contents of the tabernacle. Following this, in chapter 38, the tabernacle is called the Tabernacle of Testimony. The tabernacle could be a testimony of God in Christ because of its contents. Likewise, the church could be a testimony of God in Christ because the church has Christ as its contents.

THE SURPLUS OF THE EXPERIENCE OF CHRIST AS THE MATERIAL FOR BUILDING THE CHURCH

Exodus 38:21-31 goes on to speak of the primary materials used for making the contents of the tabernacle. The materials mentioned in this portion are the gold, the silver, and the bronze. In chapter 35 we saw that all the materials with which the tabernacle and its furniture were made are types of the different aspects of Christ experienced by us. When we experience Christ in a certain aspect, we have something of Christ as a surplus to offer to God. The materials typify the aspects of Christ experienced by us and the surplus of that experience which we bring to God as an offering. The surplus becomes the material with which the tabernacle and its furniture are constructed.

The church could be built up only with the different aspects of Christ experienced by us and brought as a surplus to God. If we do not experience Christ in an adequate way and to a full extent, there will not be sufficient material for the building of the church.

The record of the sum of the gold, silver, and bronze indicates that there was a surplus (Exo. 38:24-29). With the gold there was the surplus (v. 24). With the silver there was also a surplus. Verse 25 says, "The silver of those who were numbered of the assembly was one hundred talents and one thousand seven hundred seventy-five shekels, according to the shekel of the sanctuary." In addition to the one hundred talents there was a surplus. The bronze was also in the same principle (v. 29). The record of these quantities indicates that the materials signify the things of Christ experienced by us. They are not the things created by God in predetermined amounts. If they were merely something created and determined by God, there would be no surplus. One hundred talents would be one hundred talents, without a surplus. But with each of these items, the sum of the weight contains a surplus, a remainder, representing something experienced by us and offered to God.

If the people of Israel had not possessed enough silver and had not been able to offer much, the materials for the building of the tabernacle would have been lacking. The amount of the weight of the silver was according to the number of the people. Verse 26 says, "A beka a head, that is, half a shekel, according to the shekel of the sanctuary, for each one who was enrolled among their numbering, from twenty years old and upward, for six hundred three thousand, five hundred fifty men." From each person came half a shekel. If there had been fewer people, the amount of the silver would have been less. In that case, the silver would not have been sufficient for the tabernacle. The less experience the people of God have, the less material there will be for the building of the Lord's house. Less experience will produce a shortage. The material for building the church comes from the experience of Christ by the people of God. If we do not have much experience, the material for the building of the church will be in shortage.

THE ORDER OF OUR EXPERIENCE

Exodus 38:24 through 31 mentions first the gold, then the silver, and finally the bronze. However, in our experience the gold does not come first. On the contrary, the bronze comes first, then the silver, and then the gold. In the Scriptures, bronze signifies in type the tests, the trials, the judgment, and even the temptations that Christ suffered. His whole life was a life full of tests, trials, and temptations, and at the end, He was judged by God on the cross. These sufferings became the very foundation upon which Christ accomplished redemption for us. Christ accomplished redemption by being tested, tried, tempted, judged, and eventually crucified on the cross. Therefore, after the bronze comes the silver, signifying the redemption of Christ. This redemption comes from the judgment, trials, and tests suffered by Christ. Without these sufferings, Christ could never have accomplished redemption for us. The silver must come after the bronze. After the silver is the gold; that is, after the experience of the redemption of Christ is the experience of the divine nature of God. The redemption of Christ brings the divine nature into our experience. As long as we have been redeemed by Christ, we have the divine nature of God (2 Pet. 1:4). At the time when we believed into Christ as our Redeemer, we received the divine nature.

The bronze, the silver, and the gold become the material for the building of the house of God through our experience. These aspects must be experienced by us in order to become the material for the building of the church. We must experience the tests, the trials, the temptations, and the judgments that Christ suffered. We must also experience the redemption of Christ, and we must experience the divine nature of God. We can possess something of Christ as the bronze and offer it to God as material for building His house by experiencing Christ in the aspect of His test and trials. We have to be tested, tried, and judged in Christ. Many times God will put us into tests, trials, and sufferings in order that we may experience something of Christ.

In the same principle, we must experience the redemption of Christ. Much is involved with Christ's redemption. Sin was dealt with by the cross, by the shedding of the Lord's blood (John 1:29; 1 Pet. 2:24). The world, the evil one, the kingdom of darkness, and the old man with the natural life have also been dealt with on the cross (Gal. 6:14; Heb. 2:14; John 12:31;

Rom. 6:6). We need to experience the Christ who was crucified, shedding His blood to wash away our sins and dealing with the old man, the natural life, the world, the kingdom of darkness, and all things which are against God and His purpose. This experience of the redemption of Christ becomes something that we can offer to God as the material for the building up of the church. If we do not experience the redemption, the cross of Christ, in such a full and adequate way, we will not have sufficient silver to offer to the Lord for His building.

As we have pointed out, the amount of silver offered was according to the number of the people of Israel (Exo. 38:26). If there had been fewer men numbered, there would not have been enough silver for the material for the tabernacle. If there is not a sufficient number of believers among us, there will be a shortage of the material for the building of the church. We need to increase the number of the people by bringing others to experience the redemption of Christ. We have to preach the gospel to increase the number, bearing the spiritual children and bringing them into the church, the household of God. If there are a sufficient number of people experiencing the redemption of Christ, there will be enough silver as the material for the building of the tabernacle. The silver as the material for the building of the tabernacle absolutely depends on the number of people. If we do not preach the gospel to increase the number of the believers by begetting spiritual children, we will be too few in number, and there will be a shortage of silver as the material for the building of the church.

If we experience Christ's redemption, we will also experience the divine nature of God. If we have the silver, then we will have the gold. If we experience the cross, the redemption of Christ, the crucifixion of Christ with the crucifixion of the old man, the old nature, the natural life, the world, the evil powers, and the kingdom of darkness, we will be in a position to experience the divine nature. We will have the gold that we can offer to the Lord for His building.

THE FOUNDATION AND MANIFESTATION
OF THE TABERNACLE

Exodus 38:29-31 says, "The bronze of the wave offering

was seventy talents, and two thousand four hundred shekels. And with it he made the sockets for the entrance of the Tent of Meeting...and the sockets around the court and the sockets of the gate of the court and all the pegs of the tabernacle and all the pegs around the court." Verse 27 says, "The hundred talents of silver were for casting the sockets of the sanctuary and the sockets of the veil; one hundred sockets for the hundred talents, a talent for a socket." The primary use of the bronze was as a base, a foundation. Likewise, the silver was also mainly used for the base and support of the tabernacle. The hangings surrounding the outer court were based on bronze sockets (v. 31), and all the boards and the pillars of the tabernacle were based on the silver sockets and had silver hooks and connecting rods (vv. 27-28). This indicates that all the experiences of the tests, the trials, the temptations, and the judgment that Christ suffered, and all the experiences of the redemption of Christ are something for the foundation, for the base, of the building of the church. The more we experience the tests and the trials that Christ suffered, and the more we experience the redemption that Christ accomplished, the more we will have something for the foundation of the building of the church.

We must have all the experiences of the suffering of Christ and of the redemption accomplished by Christ as the foundation for the building of the church, and we must also have the experience of God's nature as the manifestation of what God is. When people come to the church, the first thing that they should see is the manifestation of God's glorious nature, typified by the gold upon the boards of the tabernacle. Whoever would go into the tabernacle would immediately see the shining gold. Likewise, anyone who comes into the church must see something of God's divine nature shining among us, the manifestation of the divine nature as typified by the gold. This manifestation of the divine nature is based upon the experiences of the sufferings of Christ and the redemption accomplished by Christ. We have to experience Christ as the bronze, the silver, and the gold so that we may have something to offer as material for the building.

In the picture of the tabernacle the foundation of the outer court is bronze. Outside the tabernacle, in the outer court, were the attacks of rain and wind. To stand against and suffer every kind of attack, the foundation of the outer court needed the bronze as its material. However, under the boards of the tabernacle itself there were sockets of silver. This does not indicate the suffering but rather the redemption of the cross. From the redemption of the cross comes the divine nature of God. All the gold that overlaid the boards was based upon the silver sockets. In the experiences of the believers, the silver follows the bronze, and the gold follows the silver. The redemption of Christ comes from the sufferings of Christ, and the experience of the divine nature is based upon the redemption of Christ.

CHAPTER TWELVE

THE FELLOWSHIP OF THE BODY AND
THE PRIESTLY GARMENTS

Scripture Reading: Exo. 39:1-31; 36:8, 14, 19

Exodus 39 is a record of the making of the garments of the priests. The holy garments with the shoulder pieces and the breastplate of gold and precious stones signify the fellowship of the Body of Christ brought in through the priestly ministry. By this fellowship the Lord's people can minister to the Lord and minister to His people, and by this fellowship the mind, the thought, and the will of God concerning His people are revealed.

The people of the Lord are a kingdom of priests (19:6). First Peter 2:5 says, "You yourselves also, as living stones, are being built up as a spiritual house into a holy priesthood to offer up spiritual sacrifices acceptable to God through Jesus Christ." All the living stones for the building of God's spiritual house are priests. The spiritual house of God is the building up of a group of priests, and this building up is the priesthood. The priests are the members of the Body of Christ, and the priesthood is the Body. The garments upon the priests signify the fellowship of the Body of Christ brought in through the priestly ministry. The fellowship of the Body of Christ is the reality of the building up of the Body and is an issue of the building up of the Body. If there is the real building up of the Body, there must be the fellowship. The fellowship of the Body comes out of the building up of the Body.

The priesthood and the house of God provide a picture. All the priests are the materials, the living stones, for the building of the house of God, so the house of God is simply the composition of all the priests built together. The priests built together are the Body, and the garments upon the priests represent the fellowship of the Body brought in through the priestly ministry as an issue of the Body and as something built with the Body. In this fellowship of the Body there is the ministry to God and to His people and the revelation of God about His people.

THE BUILDING UP OF THE FELLOWSHIP

The making of the garments in Exodus 39 shows us that the fellowship of the Body is something built up. The blue, purple, and scarlet strands and fine twined linen were woven together in the garments. To be woven together simply means to be built together. Furthermore, verse 6 and verses 8 through 14 speak of the precious stones set in gold settings. The setting of the stones also indicates a building. The fellowship of the Body of Christ, the fellowship among the Lord's children and between God and His children, is something built up. We have to build up this fellowship.

The priestly garments were made of blue, purple, and scarlet strands and fine twined linen. Linen represents righteousness before God, even the righteousness of God. The fellowship of the Body of Christ is something constructed of the righteousness of God. The divine righteousness, the righteousness of God, is Christ Himself. Christ Himself is the fine linen. The number two signifies testimony, so the linen being twined, or doubled, indicates that the testimony of Christ as the righteousness of God is always strong. The color blue represents heavenliness, purple signifies kingship, royalty, and scarlet signifies the redeeming work of the cross. The fellowship of the Body of Christ is composed of Christ Himself as the righteousness of God with heavenliness, kingship, royalty, and the redeeming work of the cross.

Verse 4 says, "They made shoulder pieces for it, joined to it; at the two edges it was joined." Verse 8 goes on to say, "He made the breastplate, the work of a skillful workman, like the work of the ephod, of gold, of blue and purple and scarlet strands and of fine twined linen." The two shoulder pieces and the breastplate were built upon the foundation of the garment composed of the riches of Christ with heavenliness, kingship, and the redemption of the cross. The shoulder pieces and the breastplate were made with precious stones and gold. Gold, as we have seen, signifies the divine nature of God. The divine nature of God should be experienced by us to be the material for the building up of the fellowship of the Body. Precious stones represent the appearance, the likeness, the image, of God. When God reveals Himself in the Scriptures, there is the appearance of precious stones (24:10; Rev. 4:3). In our experience, this appearance comes out of the transforming work of the Holy Spirit. Precious stones are not natural materials created by God; they are created materials transformed into another kind of material. We must be transformed. The Holy Spirit works with us and transforms us into the likeness, the appearance, the image, of the Lord (2 Cor. 3:18). After being transformed, we become the precious stones, and we have the appearance, the likeness, the image, of God. The precious stones were set in gold settings, indicating that transformation is something set in the divine nature of God. We must be built up with the divine nature of God and with the transforming work of the Holy Spirit, which are the means, the instrument, for the fellowship of God's people brought in through the priestly ministry.

THE POMEGRANATES AND THE BELLS

Exodus 39:24-26 says, "They made on the hem of the robe pomegranates of blue and purple and scarlet strands, twined. And they made bells of pure gold and put the bells between the pomegranates on the hem of the robe all around, between the pomegranates; a bell and a pomegranate, a bell and a pomegranate, on the hem of the robe all around, to minister in; as Jehovah had commanded Moses." On the hem of the priestly robe were pomegranates and bells. Pomegranates, in type, signify the riches and the beauty of life. If you would look at a pomegranate, you would see that it is full of life and full of the beauty of life. The pomegranates help us to realize that there is something of life upon the priestly garments. The fellowship of the Body of Christ must be full of the riches of life and the beauty of life.

The bells, on the other hand, represent our words, our

voices of testimony, and the things we preach. With the fellowship of the Body of Christ there are always the words, the voices, and the songs as a testimony, as a message preached continually. At the hem of the robe of the garments there were the pomegranates and the golden bells, showing that with the fellowship of the Body of Christ there are always the riches and the beauty of life with the voices, with the words, as the messages of the testimony of God. Moreover, the bells were made of gold. All the messages we give, all the words, the utterances, and the voices of our testimony, and all the songs we make must be something divine, of God's divine nature. Between the golden bells were the pomegranates, and between the pomegranates were the bells. The riches and the beauty of life go together with the testimony, the voices, the sounds, of the divine nature.

On the top of the priestly garments were the precious stones and the gold built up together as the shoulder pieces and the breastplate for the ministry of the Lord and for the revelation of God, and at the bottom, on the hem of the robe, were the pomegranates and the bells for the testimony of the divine nature with the riches and beauty of life. The garments signify, on the one hand, a ministry, and on the other hand, a testimony. These are both components of the fellowship of the Body of Christ. By this fellowship we can minister to the Lord and to the Lord's people and have the revelation of the Lord concerning His people, and by this fellowship we can also give to people a testimony full of the riches and the beauty of life with the divine nature. On the one hand, every time we come together to have a meeting, there must always be, before God, the shoulder pieces and the breastplate of precious stones set in gold settings. On the other hand, before man there must also be the pomegranates and the bells, the riches and the beauty of life with the voices of testimony and the sounding of the words of the message of God.

THE PLATE OF THE HOLY CROWN

Exodus 39:30 says, "They made the plate of the holy crown of pure gold and wrote an inscription upon it, like the engravings of a signet: HOLINESS TO JEHOVAH." The plate of the crown was fastened to the turban on the head of the high priest (v. 31). It was a label placed on the high priest. Actually, this label belonged to the holy garments as a whole. The garments, as we have seen, signify the fellowship of the Body of Christ with the ministry to God and to His people. This label signifies that the fellowship of the Body with the ministry and the testimony among the Lord's children is something absolutely holy. The pure gold signifies that the holiness of the fellowship of the Lord's children is something composed of the divine nature of God.

The priestly garments were woven, or wrought, not only with fine linen but also with gold thread. The gold thread is mentioned as the first material for the garments, and the fine linen is second (v. 2). Verse 3 says, "They beat the gold into thin sheets and cut them into threads, to work into the blue and into the purple and into the scarlet strands and into the fine linen, the work of a skillful workman." The ephod and the breastplate were made of gold and linen woven together (vv. 2, 8). Furthermore, on the shoulder pieces and the breastplate precious stones were set in gold settings. The gold of the priestly garments signifies that the fellowship among the Lord's children is something of the divine nature.

The flow of the water of life in the middle of the golden street of the New Jerusalem signifies the fellowship of the holy city (Rev. 22:1; 21:21). This shows us again that the fellowship among the Lord's children is in the divine nature and of the divine life. Because this fellowship is something divine, it is holy. Only the divine things are holy. The divine nature of God is holy. Thus, the plate of the holy crown was made of pure gold and engraved with the words HOLINESS TO JEHOVAH.

THE TWO CHARACTERISTICS OF GOD'S BUILDING

Exodus 39:32-43, as a conclusion to chapters 35 through 39, is a record of all the things made by the people of Israel for the tabernacle. In these verses and in chapter 40, two different terms are used for God's building: the tabernacle and the Tent of Meeting. It is difficult to discover the significance of the meaning of these two terms. Actually, the tabernacle is the tent; these are two terms or titles for one entity. With the tabernacle, the emphasis is the dwelling place, the habitation, of God. With the tent, the significance is the place where God's people meet. The tabernacle points to the place where God dwells, but the tent points to the place where God's people meet together.

Apparently, the dwelling place of God and the priesthood are two different things. But as we have seen, the priests are the living stones, the materials, for the house of God (1 Pet. 2:5). The building of the house of God is the body of the priests. The priests are coordinated together to form a body, and this body is the building. In God's original intention, all the people of God are priests. As the priests, the people of God are the materials for the building of the dwelling place of God, and when they are coordinated and composed together, they become the dwelling place of God. Therefore, on the one hand, God's building is a tabernacle as a dwelling place, a habitation for God, and on the other hand, it is a tent as a meeting place and a composition of the Lord's children. Everything positive is here in this composition. Christ is here, the church is here, the fellowship is here, the ministry is here, and the revelation is here. This portion of chapter 40 is actually a summary of the entire tabernacle with its furniture, showing us the building as the composition of all the Lord's children.

If you will compare the items of the building listed in 39:32-43 to all the items in the foregoing chapters, you will find that two items are not mentioned here. These are the curtains of fine linen and the covering of goats' hair. The coverings of rams' skins and porpoise skins are mentioned in verse 34, but the first two layers of the covering are not mentioned by name. Strictly speaking, the curtains of fine linen and of goats' hair are the tabernacle and the tent. Verses 32 through 34 say, "Thus all the work of the tabernacle of the Tent of Meeting was finished...And they brought the tabernacle to Moses, the tent and all its furnishings, its clasps, its boards, its bars, and its pillars and its sockets; and the covering of rams' skins dyed red and the covering of porpoise skins, and the veil of the screen." *Its,* mentioned six times in verse 33, refers to the tabernacle and the tent. All the other items mentioned are the furniture of the tabernacle and the tent. With this understanding, verse 33 could read, "And they brought *the curtains of fine linen* to Moses, *the curtains of goats' hair,* and all its furnishings, its clasps, its boards, its bars, and its pillars and its sockets." All the "its" in this verse are the items belonging to the curtains of fine linen and the covering of goats' hair as the tabernacle and the tent.

Exodus 36:8 says of the curtains of fine linen, "All the wise in heart among those who did the work made the tabernacle with ten curtains, of fine twined linen and blue and purple and scarlet strands." The construction of this sentence shows that the curtains of fine linen are the tabernacle; they made the tabernacle with ten curtains. Verse 14 continues, "He made curtains of goats' hair for a tent over the tabernacle, eleven curtains he made in all." The first layer, the ten curtains of fine linen, is called the tabernacle. The second layer, the covering made of goats' hair, is called the tent. Verse 19 says, "He made a covering for the tent, of rams' skins dyed red, and a covering of porpoise skins above it." The tabernacle is the curtains of fine linen, the tent over the tabernacle is the covering of goats' hair, and the rams' skins are the covering over the tent. The reason why the first two layers of coverings are not mentioned in 39:33-34 is because these two coverings are the tabernacle and the tent.

Now we may understand what the difference between the tabernacle and the tent is. From within, it is the tabernacle, the dwelling place of God, and from without, it is the tent, the meeting place of God's people. The inner layer is the tabernacle, and the outer layer is the tent. These two layers are the basic components; all the other items belong to them. The church is the building, the composition of God's people. From within, it is the dwelling place of God, and from without, it is the meeting place of the Lord's children. These are the two characteristics of the building of God.

ABOUT THE AUTHOR

Witness Lee was born in 1905 in northern China and raised in a Christian family. At age 19 he was fully captured for Christ and immediately consecrated himself to preach the gospel for the rest of his life. Early in his service, he met Watchman Nee, a renowned preacher, teacher, and writer. Witness Lee labored together with Watchman Nee under his direction. In 1934 Watchman Nee entrusted Witness Lee with the responsibility for his publication operation, called the Shanghai Gospel Bookroom.

Prior to the Communist takeover in 1949, Witness Lee was sent by Watchman Nee and his other co-workers to Taiwan to ensure that the things delivered to them by the Lord would not be lost. Watchman Nee instructed Witness Lee to continue the former's publishing operation abroad as the Taiwan Gospel Bookroom, which has been publicly recognized as the publisher of Watchman Nee's works outside China. Witness Lee's work in Taiwan manifested the Lord's abundant blessing. From a mere 350 believers, newly fled from the mainland, the churches in Taiwan grew to 20,000 in five years.

In 1962 Witness Lee felt led of the Lord to come to the United States, settling in California. During his 35 years of service in the U.S., he ministered in weekly meetings and weekend conferences, delivering several thousand spoken messages. Much of his speaking has since been published as over 400 titles. Many of these have been translated into over fourteen languages. He gave his last public conference in February 1997 at the age of 91.

He leaves behind a prolific presentation of the truth in the Bible. His major work, *Life-study of the Bible,* comprises over 25,000 pages of commentary on every book of the Bible from the perspective of the believers' enjoyment and experience of God's divine life in Christ through the Holy Spirit. Witness Lee was the chief editor of a new translation of the New Testament into Chinese called the Recovery Version and directed the translation of the same into English. The Recovery Version also appears in a number of other languages. He provided an extensive body of footnotes, outlines, and spiritual cross references. A radio broadcast of his messages can be heard on Christian radio stations in the United States. In 1965 Witness Lee founded Living Stream Ministry, a non-profit corporation, located in Anaheim, California, which officially presents his and Watchman Nee's ministry.

Witness Lee's ministry emphasizes the experience of Christ as life and the practical oneness of the believers as the Body of Christ. Stressing the importance of attending to both these matters, he led the churches under his care to grow in Christian life and function. He was unbending in his conviction that God's goal is not narrow sectarianism but the Body of Christ. In time, believers began to meet simply as the church in their localities in response to this conviction. In recent years a number of new churches have been raised up in Russia and in many eastern European countries.